100
DAYS
in
THE
GOSPELS

PUBLISHING GROUP

NASHVILLE, TENNESSEE

978-1-4336-4917-2

Published by B&H Publishing Group
Nashville, Tennessee

Custom edition published for LifeWay Christian Stores.

1 2 3 4 5 6 7 • 20 19 18 17 16

Contents

Introduction

The whole Bible is the story of God's redemption of humanity through Jesus Christ. While the rest of Scripture points to Jesus, the Gospels are the narrative of His life, death, and resurrection on Earth.

If you have spent any time reading the Bible, you've most likely had at least some experience and exposure to all of the stories you are about to read; but this is a chance to focus in and meditate on the individual details Scripture gives us about the early church, and the questions and problems they faced. This devotional is meant to be a magnifying glass to help you focus in and sit in passages from the New Testament that we too often skim over and lose the full impact.

Whether you choose to read them one a day, one a week, or at whatever speed you choose, you'll be keeping the Word in the center of your thoughts and growing in your walk with Christ.

John 1:1–14
The Word

In the beginning was the Word, and the Word was with God, and the Word was God. He was with God in the beginning. All things were created through Him, and apart from Him not one thing was created that has been created. Life was in Him, and that life was the light of men. That light shines in the darkness, yet the darkness did not overcome it.

There was a man named John who was sent from God. He came as a witness to testify about the light, so that all might believe through him. He was not the light, but he came to testify about the light. The true light, who gives light to everyone, was coming into the world.

He was in the world, and the world was created through Him, yet the world did not recognize Him. He came to His own, and His own people did not receive Him. But to all who did receive Him, He gave them the right to be children of God, to those who believe in His name, who were born, not of blood, or of the will of the flesh, or of the will of man, but of God.

The Word became flesh and took up residence among us. We observed His glory, the glory as the One and Only Son from the Father, full of grace and truth.

John began his Gospel with a concise and powerful statement. "The Word" is a wonderful, descriptive title for Jesus, the Son of God. Jesus is the eternal, pre-existing Word-become-flesh. He is the direct message from the Father who reveals His purpose through the very life of Christ.

The Word (Jesus) is the Author and Creator of all things. Not one thing was made apart from Him. He was there when the Father spoke the heavens and the earth into being.

Have you ever noticed the first-person plural pronouns in Genesis 1:26? Scripture reads: "Let Us make man in Our image, according to Our likeness." It's likely that many of us imagine just God the Father present during creation. But it was the Trinity—they were all there, including Jesus, as John tells us in his Gospel. Jesus "was with God in the beginning." This gives us a bigger picture of Jesus' role. He didn't just begin to exist and work when He was born in Bethlehem. He has existed since the beginning.

He was there in the garden when God called out to Adam. He was there when God gave the law to Moses and dwelled among His people in the tabernacle. He was with God and He was God.

And now here Jesus is, the culmination of the Father's plan for salvation. The One who made everything, from the highest angel to the lowliest ant, is now here to be our salvation—the Author and Finisher of our faith. Who else is more qualified to offer new life than the One who created life? God gave us His Word, and this is good news indeed!

Luke 1:1–4
Confirming the Truth

Many have undertaken to compile a narrative about the events that have been fulfilled among us, just as the original eyewitnesses and servants of the word handed them down to us. It also seemed good to me, since I have carefully investigated everything from the very first, to write to you in an orderly sequence, most honorable Theophilus, so that you may know the certainty of the things about which you have been instructed.

Children know what they believe because it's what their parents tell them to believe. Youngsters initially believe their parents because they love and trust them. But as those children get older, they need to confirm the truth for themselves.

This is true for all children, regardless of their parents' religious affiliations (or lack thereof), but it is especially true for children of believers. For all of us, this movement from received faith to convictional faith requires study and instruction. Doesn't personal holiness require mental perspiration as it does spiritual inspiration?

We need to be certain of what Scripture says and what it tells us is true so that we can testify to it when confronted by those who challenge us. And we will be challenged. Satan started challenging the truthfulness of God in the first pages of Genesis when he tempted Eve in the garden, causing her to question what God Himself had told her.

The world around us continually strives to undermine each foundational doctrine we hold dear. We must stand up when others stand against what our Bible teaches. We can only do this when we are certain of what it does teach.

For this reason, the Holy Spirit called and inspired Luke to write the third Gospel. By verse 4, we are several lines into what will be a two-volume work, Luke and Acts. These works are the church history books of the New Testament. They cover the life of Jesus and the spread of the early church. In verse 4, Luke tells us the purpose of his church history. He wrote it for his friend Theophilus, so he would be certain of the things he had learned about the life and ministry of Jesus. We can also have this certainty by confirming what we have heard with careful study and by understanding Scripture and the life of Jesus as a whole.

Luke's Gospel is intended to equip us to confidently live out the incredibly good news of Jesus and to tell the gospel knowledgeably to others.

Luke 1:26–38
May It Be Done

In the sixth month, the angel Gabriel was sent by God to a town in Galilee called Nazareth, to a virgin engaged to a man named Joseph, of the house of David. The virgin's name was Mary. And the angel came to her and said, "Rejoice, favored woman! The Lord is with you." But she was deeply troubled by this statement, wondering what kind of greeting this could be. Then the angel told her:

"Do not be afraid, Mary, for you have found favor with God. Now listen: You will conceive and give birth to a son, and you will call His name Jesus. He will be great and will be called the Son of the Most High, and the Lord God will give Him the throne of His father David. He will reign over the house of Jacob forever, and His kingdom will have no end."

Mary asked the angel, "How can this be, since I have not been intimate with a man?"

The angel replied to her:

"The Holy Spirit will come upon you, and the power of the Most High will overshadow you. Therefore, the holy One to be born will be called the Son of God.

"And consider your relative Elizabeth—even she has conceived a son in her old age, and this is the sixth month for her who was called childless. For nothing will be impossible with God."

"I am the Lord's slave," said Mary. "May it be done to me according to your word." Then the angel left her.

Imagine a teenage girl just minding her own business when an angel suddenly appears and tells her God is with her. Scripture tells us that young Mary was deeply troubled when that happened to her, and with good cause. It wasn't something that happened every day!

The angel continued with a proclamation that was confusing. Mary was going to have a baby, and that baby would be the Son of God. What?!

"How can this be, since I have not been intimate with a man?" Mary said. It's interesting that her only confusion was about how she could get pregnant without having sex, not that her baby would be the Son of God.

The angel continued by explaining how it would happen, and that something similarly miraculous had happened to her elderly cousin Elizabeth.

Then this teenage girl basically said, in today's vernacular, "Okay. That's cool. Whatever you say." Again, what?!

If an angel came to you with such a seemingly outlandish proposition, what would you say? How would you react? It's really hard to know. But when we look at the passage, we see that the angel didn't ask Mary if this plan was all right with her. He just told her it was going to happen. And she went with it.

Are we as eager to go with it when God tells us or shows us what He wants us to do? Do we try to resist and make excuses why we can't do it, or do we say, with Mary, "May it be done to me according to your word"?

Luke 1:39–55
A Song of Praise

*In those days Mary set out and hurried to a town
in the hill country of Judah where she entered
Zechariah's house and greeted Elizabeth. When
Elizabeth heard Mary's greeting, the baby leaped
inside her, and Elizabeth was filled with the Holy
Spirit. Then she exclaimed with a loud cry:*

*"You are the most blessed of women, and your
child will be blessed!*

*How could this happen to me, that the mother
of my Lord should come to me? For you see, when
the sound of your greeting reached my ears,
the baby leaped for joy inside me! She who has
believed is blessed because what was spoken to
her by the Lord will be fulfilled!"*

And Mary said:

*"My soul proclaims the greatness of the Lord,
and my spirit has rejoiced in God my Savior,
because He has looked with favor on the humble
condition of His slave. Surely, from now on all generations will call me blessed, because the Mighty
One has done great things for me, and His name is
holy. His mercy is from generation to generation on
those who fear Him. He has done a mighty deed
with His arm; He has scattered the proud because
of the thoughts of their hearts; He has toppled the*

mighty from their thrones and exalted the lowly. He has satisfied the hungry with good things and sent the rich away empty. He has helped His servant Israel, mindful of His mercy, just as He spoke to our ancestors, to Abraham and his descendants forever."

M ary had an exceedingly great reason to praise the Lord because she was chosen to bring forth a baby who would be the Savior of the World. Her song resonated with a spirit of awe and humility before her Lord. She showed us a glimpse into her heart of worship as she sang many accolades of praise, which listed God's wondrous ways.

Praise like this comes from a heart in close relationship with God. Those who walk with the Lord continually and wholly seek Him and His ways. They know through life experiences that what Scripture proclaims about God is true. They have seen God at work, and their lives become a song of praise. They are unable to keep from praising Him, and they can't help but tell others about who He is and what He has done.

Do you long to see up close and personal the magnificent works of our Almighty God? Is your heart fully surrendered and yielded to God? Does a song of praise easily flow from your mouth? Ask God to fill you with praise for His mighty works today.

Matthew 1:18–23
God With Us

The birth of Jesus Christ came about this way: After His mother Mary had been engaged to Joseph, it was discovered before they came together that she was pregnant by the Holy Spirit. So her husband Joseph, being a righteous man, and not wanting to disgrace her publicly, decided to divorce her secretly.

But after he had considered these things, an angel of the Lord suddenly appeared to him in a dream, saying, "Joseph, son of David, don't be afraid to take Mary as your wife, because what has been conceived in her is by the Holy Spirit. She will give birth to a son, and you are to name Him Jesus, because He will save His people from their sins."

Now all this took place to fulfill what was spoken by the Lord through the prophet: See, the virgin will become pregnant and give birth to a son, and they will name Him Immanuel, which is translated "God is with us."

Y ou may have a mental list of places you would love to visit—an exotic island, a culturally rich city, a place where ancient ruins make history come alive, or a scenic gem. Perhaps you'd like to see the land of your ancestors or the setting of a favorite book or movie.

Or maybe you want to go to the Holy Land and walk where Jesus and Paul walked.

On the other hand, there are likely some places you would never want to visit—perhaps because of terror threats, or maybe because it would bring up painful memories. You might want to avoid a certain person who lives there. Or maybe the country is an unsafe place for Christians or people of your race or skin tone.

Maybe you live in a place that is so amazing that you see no reason to go anywhere else, because nothing could compare to your home. If you live in a safe place that anyone would consider to be a paradise, you would seemingly have no desire to go to somewhere with less appeal—unless you're going there to visit someone you love and care about deeply.

That's exactly what Jesus did when He came to Earth. If we don't acknowledge what He left behind, then it is difficult to grasp the significance of His coming here and why He made that choice. The name Immanuel proclaims Jesus' deity. God Himself left heaven—the one place that trumps every other place on your list of places to visit combined—to come to this sin-filled earth full of people who would hate Him and ultimately kill Him. There was nothing here He needed to see up close, because He had created it all. He came because He loves us. He wanted to walk among us and, ultimately, to take us to that better place from which He had come.

Luke 2:1–14
Gloria in Excelsis Deo!

In those days a decree went out from Caesar Augustus that the whole empire should be registered. This first registration took place while Quirinius was governing Syria. So everyone went to be registered, each to his own town.

And Joseph also went up from the town of Nazareth in Galilee, to Judea, to the city of David, which is called Bethlehem, because he was of the house and family line of David, to be registered along with Mary, who was engaged to him and was pregnant. While they were there, the time came for her to give birth. Then she gave birth to her firstborn Son, and she wrapped Him snugly in cloth and laid Him in a feeding trough—because there was no room for them at the lodging place.

In the same region, shepherds were staying out in the fields and keeping watch at night over their flock. Then an angel of the Lord stood before them, and the glory of the Lord shone around them, and they were terrified. But the angel said to them, "Don't be afraid, for look, I proclaim to you good news of great joy that will be for all the people: Today a Savior, who is Messiah the Lord, was born for you in the city of David. This will be the sign for you: You will find a baby wrapped snugly in cloth and lying in a feeding trough."

Suddenly there was a multitude of the heavenly host with the angel, praising God and saying:
Glory to God in the highest heaven, and peace on earth to people He favors!

We literally sing Luke 2:14 when we sing about the angels we have heard on high and "Gloria in Excelsis Deo," which is Latin for "Glory to God in the highest." That heavenly host of angels gave honor to our Lord in one exclamation of praise.

But Jesus' birth didn't give glory to God that He didn't already possess. Instead, the angels were proclaiming the incredible, magnificent glory that has been and will continue to be His forever. The coming of Jesus demonstrated God's glory in the most magnificent way. When we celebrate Jesus' birth at Christmas, we join the angels in that confession.

God's glory was only part of the message. His people had been waiting for the Messiah to bring them peace. But the peace found in God's glory through Jesus Christ is not earthly peace; it is everlasting peace with God. Those who place their faith in Jesus receive God's eternal grace.

What is the meaning of that first Christmas day for you? Are you still looking for God to prove His glory, or have you recognized the fullness of it through a relationship with His Son, Christ Jesus?

Luke 2:15–20

What They Had Seen and Heard

When the angels had left them and returned to heaven, the shepherds said to one another, "Let's go straight to Bethlehem and see what has happened, which the Lord has made known to us."

They hurried off and found both Mary and Joseph, and the baby who was lying in the feeding trough. After seeing them, they reported the message they were told about this child, and all who heard it were amazed at what the shepherds said to them. But Mary was treasuring up all these things in her heart and meditating on them. The shepherds returned, glorifying and praising God for all they had seen and heard, just as they had been told.

In this media-frenzied world, nothing gets our attention like an eyewitness report. We like to hear from the people who are—or were—on the scene. It improves credibility. If we didn't see and hear it ourselves, we want to get the news from someone who did. It satisfies our desire to be there ourselves.

The shepherds didn't disappoint. The angel of the Lord told them what to expect. After the angel and the rest of the heavenly host had left, they decided to go see for themselves. When they confirmed it, they set out to tell others. What they had been told matched what they had seen. They must have been convincing, because the Bible says all who heard it were amazed.

Nineteenth century pastor Charles Spurgeon points out the connection between what the shepherds had seen and heard:

> One point for which [the shepherds] praised God was the agreement between what they had heard and what they had seen. Observe the last sentence—"As it was told unto them." Have you not found the gospel to be in yourselves just what the Bible said it would be? . . . Surely what we have "seen" keeps pace with, nay, far exceeds, what we have "heard." Let us, then, glorify and praise God for a Saviour so precious, and so satisfying.

When the shepherds had told the good news of Jesus to others, they returned to their fields, paying tribute to the Source, glorifying and praising the heavenly Father for all they had seen and heard.

People are longing to hear the news from people they believe and trust. If the shepherds could do this, think what you can do. Who can you tell about what Jesus did on the cross and what you have witnessed Him doing in your life and the lives of others?

Quote: Charles Spurgeon, *Morning and Evening*, January 28.

Luke 2:41–52
Lost and Found

Every year His parents traveled to Jerusalem for the Passover Festival. When He was 12 years old, they went up according to the custom of the festival. After those days were over, as they were returning, the boy Jesus stayed behind in Jerusalem, but His parents did not know it. Assuming He was in the traveling party, they went a day's journey. Then they began looking for Him among their relatives and friends. When they did not find Him, they returned to Jerusalem to search for Him. After three days, they found Him in the temple complex sitting among the teachers, listening to them and asking them questions. And all those who heard Him were astounded at His understanding and His answers. When His parents saw Him, they were astonished, and His mother said to Him, "Son, why have You treated us like this? Your father and I have been anxiously searching for You."

"Why were you searching for Me?" He asked them. "Didn't you know that I had to be in My Father's house?" But they did not understand what He said to them.

Then He went down with them and came to Nazareth and was obedient to them. His mother kept all these things in her heart. And Jesus

increased in wisdom and stature, and in favor with
God and with people.

How could Mary and Joseph not know their child was missing for an entire day? Likely, everyone thought He was with someone else. We know they were in a "traveling party," which could have been made up of hundreds of people. Additionally, it is possible that the women and children traveled in one party, followed by the men. A twelve-year-old boy was at just the age where He could have been part of either group.

Regardless of how He was left behind without anyone noticing, Jesus was still in Jerusalem. But how were they to find him? At the time, up to a hundred thousand people lived in Jerusalem, and another several hundred thousand would have been there for the Feast of the Passover. It's frankly amazing they found Him as quickly as they did.

We read that Mary and Joseph were astonished when they saw Him, but Jesus was astonished that they hadn't known where to find Him. But His parents didn't understand why He was there, how He knew the things He was discussing with the teachers, or the meaning of His explanation of why He was there. This gives us a pretty good indication that Jesus' childhood was a fairly normal one for a child. He obviously hadn't been performing miracles or doing other supernatural things, as some early Christian writings claimed, or His parents wouldn't have been surprised by His actions.

Instead, we are told that He grew "in wisdom and stature, and in favor with God and with people" (2:52). This is a good reminder that while Jesus was fully God, He was also fully human. He grew as children naturally grow up—mentally, physically, and spiritually.

Matthew 2:13–23
Fulfilling the Prophecies

After they were gone, an angel of the Lord suddenly appeared to Joseph in a dream, saying, "Get up! Take the child and His mother, flee to Egypt, and stay there until I tell you. For Herod is about to search for the child to destroy Him." So he got up, took the child and His mother during the night, and escaped to Egypt. He stayed there until Herod's death, so that what was spoken by the Lord through the prophet might be fulfilled: Out of Egypt I called My Son.

Then Herod, when he saw that he had been outwitted by the wise men, flew into a rage. He gave orders to massacre all the male children in and around Bethlehem who were two years old and under, in keeping with the time he had learned from the wise men. Then what was spoken through Jeremiah the prophet was fulfilled: A voice was heard in Ramah, weeping, and great mourning, Rachel weeping for her children; and she refused to be consoled, because they were no more.

After Herod died, an angel of the Lord suddenly appeared in a dream to Joseph in Egypt, saying, "Get up! Take the child and His mother and go to the land of Israel, because those who sought the child's life are dead." So he got up, took the child and His mother, and entered the land of Israel. But when he heard that Archelaus was ruling over Judea in place of his father Herod, he was afraid to go there. And being warned in a dream, he withdrew to the region of Galilee. Then he went and settled in a town called Nazareth to fulfill what was spoken through the prophets, that He will be called a Nazarene.

When this passage is studied or taught, typically the focus is on Joseph's obedience in immediately doing what the angel of the Lord told him to do. And that's not a bad point of concentration. There is some great life application to be found here.

However, what is often overlooked is that in the events of these few verses, three Old Testament prophecies were fulfilled. We typically just skip past it, because we're looking at it from two millennia in the future.

But to the Jewish people in Matthew's day, this was a huge deal. The religious leaders knew the Scriptures backward and forward. Those who already believed that Jesus was the Christ could point to those prophecies as evidence that Jesus was truly the Messiah. Those who were skeptical would have had a hard time denying that He was the fulfillment of those prophecies.

Matthew was making it clear that this was the One the people of Israel had been waiting for. In fact, the preceding verses include two other fulfilled prophecies about Jesus, and the ones immediately following point out a prophecy fulfilled by John the Baptist.

Jesus' story does not stand in isolation. We read about Him throughout Scripture—not just in the New Testament. His life and work permeate God's Word, and they should permeate our lives.

Matthew 3:1–6, 11–12
Uncommon Commitment

*In those days John the Baptist came, preaching
in the Wilderness of Judea and saying, "Repent,
because the kingdom of heaven has come near!"
For he is the one spoken of through the prophet
Isaiah, who said: "A voice of one crying out in the
wilderness: Prepare the way for the Lord; make His
paths straight!"*

*John himself had a camel-hair garment with
a leather belt around his waist, and his food
was locusts and wild honey. Then people from
Jerusalem, all Judea, and all the vicinity of the
Jordan were flocking to him, and they were bap-
tized by him in the Jordan River as they confessed
their sins. . . .*

*"I baptize you with water for repentance, but
the One who is coming after me is more powerful
than I. I am not worthy to remove His sandals. He
Himself will baptize you with the Holy Spirit and
fire. His winnowing shovel is in His hand, and He
will clear His threshing floor and gather His wheat
into the barn. But the chaff He will burn up with fire
that never goes out."*

In October 1958, Elisabeth Elliot and her daughter relocated to
the wilderness of eastern Ecuador to live among the Auca tribe.

Until that time, no outsiders had been able to interact with the fierce, unreached people without losing their lives. In fact, just years earlier, Elisabeth's husband and four other missionaries had been speared to death by the Auca.

Yet Elisabeth knew the importance of bringing the gospel message to this feared people, and she succeeded. For two years, she ministered to the same tribesmen who had killed her husband. Other missionaries followed, and many of the Auca people (now called Waodani) have become believers in Jesus Christ. They are no longer the feared, murderous tribe they were sixty years ago.

Truly an amazing missionary, Elisabeth displayed uncommon dedication. She sacrificed much for the cause of Christ. There is no doubt the Auca thought she was a strange person and a brave one. Who would do such a thing as live among her husband's murderers?

John the Baptist also demonstrated uncommon commitment to the task God had created him for. He sacrificed the comforts of home and community, making the wilderness of Judea his pulpit. Filled with the Holy Spirit from birth, chosen to prepare the way for the Messiah, and privileged to baptize the Savior, John the Baptist enjoyed an extraordinary ministry. Bizarre in his diet, strange in his attire, and unique in his message, John drew people into the wilderness to hear him. He preached with great power and conviction, and many responded to his call. John chose to be different in order to point people to Jesus.

As Christians, we also are called to be unusual—light in a dark world. Do our lifestyles, words, and actions provide evidence of transformed hearts? Our mission, like John's, is to point people to Jesus.

Matthew 4:1–4
All Will Be Tempted

Then Jesus was led up by the Spirit into the wilderness to be tempted by the Devil. After He had fasted 40 days and 40 nights, He was hungry. Then the tempter approached Him and said, "If You are the Son of God, tell these stones to become bread." But He answered, "It is written: Man must not live on bread alone but on every word that comes from the mouth of God."

We often hear people say, "Stay away from the things that tempt you, and you'll be okay," or "Avoid your temptation triggers." That's not bad advice, but it's not the whole story. No matter what we do to avoid temptation, there is one who desires to draw us into sin, and he will work his wiles on even the holiest of believers. No one is above the reach of temptation. After all, Satan tempted Jesus himself.

Consider these words of nineteenth-century pastor Charles Spurgeon:

A holy character does not avert temptation—Jesus was tempted. When Satan tempts us, his sparks fall upon tinder; but in Christ's case, it was like striking sparks on water; yet the enemy continued his evil work. Now, if the devil goes on striking when there is no result, how much more will he do it when he knows what inflammable stuff our hearts are made of. . . . In the haunts of men we expect to be tempted, but even seclusion will not guard us from the same trial. Jesus Christ was led away from human society into the wilderness, and was tempted of the devil. Solitude has its charms and its benefits, and may be useful in checking the lust of the eye and the pride of life; but the devil will follow us into the most lovely retreats. Do not suppose that it is only the worldly-minded who have dreadful thoughts and blasphemous temptations, for even spiritual-minded persons endure the same; and in the holiest position we may suffer the darkest temptation. The utmost consecration of spirit will not insure you against Satanic temptation. Christ was consecrated through and through. It was his meat and drink to do the will of him that sent him: and yet he was tempted! Your hearts may glow with a seraphic flame of love to Jesus, and yet the devil will try to bring you down. . . . If you will tell me when God permits a Christian to lay aside his armour, I will tell you when Satan has left off temptation.

We will be tempted. There is no escape from it. But there is hope in the midst of temptation. When we know Scripture, we can fight the Devil's schemes with God's Word, as Jesus did. And we must put on the full Armor of Christ. Paul tells us, "In every situation take the shield of faith, and with it you will be able to extinguish all the flaming arrows of the evil one" (Eph. 6:16).

Quote: Charles Spurgeon, *Morning and Evening*, February 20.

Matthew 4:5–7
The Other Perspective

Then the Devil took Him to the holy city, had Him stand on the pinnacle of the temple, and said to Him, "If You are the Son of God, throw Yourself down. For it is written: He will give His angels orders concerning you, and they will support you with their hands so that you will not strike your foot against a stone." Jesus told him, "It is also written: Do not test the Lord your God."

Here we find Jesus at the second of three temptations by Satan. The Devil has brought Jesus to the very center of religious life, the temple in Jerusalem.

It should not surprise us that Satan knows Scripture. He often knows it better than we do. For some reason, he thought he could outwit the Word who became flesh with His own words. Even we can see that the Scripture he quoted was out of context and being improperly used. Of course, Jesus saw that, too. Instead of arguing with the Devil, Jesus simply quoted Scripture that repelled the perversion of Scripture.

When studying this second temptation, we often put ourselves in the place of Jesus. We think, "I need to know God's Word well so that I can know when Satan is twisting it." That's a great lesson to learn from this event. It's important to know God's Word so we can resist Satan's schemes to get us to sin and disrespect God. However, do we ever put ourselves in Satan's place in this story and see what lessons we can learn from that perspective?

Like the Devil, we too try to manipulate God. We do it with prayer, with empty promises, with Scripture, and with challenges. Most of us are guilty of praying a prayer similar to, "God, if You give me a better job, I'll tell all my new coworkers about You," or, "If You will just make my chronic pain go away, I'll start a ministry to help other people with this problem. I couldn't possibly do it now." Or we might use His Word to try to get Him to do something. "God, Your Word says, 'Sons are indeed a heritage from the Lord, children, a reward' (Psalm 127:3). I've followed You and served You. Therefore, You should reward me with children." Or we try to challenge or test Him, like Satan did. "God, if you're all-powerful, then get me a better job. Heal my mom. Make my kids obey me. You can do anything, after all." In our finite minds, we are trying to bargain with the infinite Creator.

God sees through our schemes as we see through the infantile requests and manipulations from children. We can't trick Him any more than Satan could trick Jesus.

We need to be honest with God with our requests. He already knows what we need, and He responds and demonstrates His love for us.

Matthew 4:8–11
No Other Gods

Again, the Devil took Him to a very high mountain and showed Him all the kingdoms of the world and their splendor. And he said to Him, "I will give You all these things if You will fall down and worship me." Then Jesus told him, "Go away, Satan! For it is written: Worship the Lord your God, and serve only Him." Then the Devil left Him, and immediately angels came and began to serve Him.

Idolatry is rampant. People seem to jump from one belief system to another on nothing but a whim or simply out of boredom. Worshipping just one god is nearly a thing of the past.

Missionaries who work with Hindu people talk about the difficulty of getting them to worship only the one true God. Many will easily accept Jesus as a "little-g" god, but they simply add Him to their collection of other deities. They figure it won't hurt to add another god to the list of those they pray to and count on for various things.

But don't many Christians do the same thing? Jesus is just another god we put on our mantel of deities. We have introduced to our daily lives other idols, other objects of worship, and other false gods to serve. The One who created all now sits quietly among the gods of this world.

"Who and what are these other gods?" you may ask. Wealth. Sports. Status. Pleasure. Television. Social media. Kids. Grandkids. Church.

"I don't worship these!" you might exclaim. Perhaps not consciously, but many of us have given in to a type of idolatry. There are some who treat sport teams and star players as objects of worship. There are those who idolize their children or grandchildren.

"But those things are important!" you say. "Especially kids!" Of course kids are important, but consider the parents who let all other relationships and ministry and attention to any semblance of a spiritual life go by the wayside because their sole focus is on their kids. Or think about the grandparents who expect their grandkids to fulfill them in a way only Jesus can.

Others idolize marriage. They think if only they were married, they'd be fulfilled. Or if only their husband or wife would do this or that, like their friend's spouse does, life would be perfect. Again, they are looking for a human to fill a spot only God should fill.

The idol that can be the hardest to spot is church, which might seem like an odd idol. But it's not uncommon for believers to look to church attendance or volunteerism as the most important thing in their lives. They seek human accolades and a feeling of accomplishment for diligently serving God instead of serving Him out of love.

Determine in your heart to make God the only god in your life. Reflect on what other things might be taking His place in your heart, and then remove them from His rightful spot.

John 1:29–37
Jesus-Promotion

The next day John saw Jesus coming toward him and said, "Here is the Lamb of God, who takes away the sin of the world! This is the One I told you about: 'After me comes a man who has surpassed me, because He existed before me.' I didn't know Him, but I came baptizing with water so He might be revealed to Israel."

And John testified, "I watched the Spirit descending from heaven like a dove, and He rested on Him. I didn't know Him, but He who sent me to baptize with water told me, 'The One you see the Spirit descending and resting on—He is the One who baptizes with the Holy Spirit.' I have seen and testified that He is the Son of God!"

Again the next day, John was standing with two of his disciples. When he saw Jesus passing by, he said, "Look! The Lamb of God!"

The two disciples heard him say this and followed Jesus.

The apostle John begins early in his Gospel giving us a record of those who testified of Jesus, particularly to His divinity. Chief among these was Jesus' cousin, John the Baptist. John knew that his ministry of preparation would wane, and this was right. Jesus must increase as He decreased. And so it should be in our own lives.

Followers of Christ know this is right. Many Christians do a good job of hiding behind the cross so that they may make much of Christ. Sadly, there are some who seem to want the attention for themselves. The lights. The platform. The applause. The praise of man. These things can easily take us off course.

A missionary recounts how a man he came to know in Asia reminded him a lot of John the Baptist. His name was Matthew. Matthew's work for the kingdom drew a lot of attention because he was so effective. The more the missionary studied the man's methods, though, the more he realized it was not the methods that made Matthew so effective; it was his character, his humility. When people were in Matthew's presence, he was always pointing them to Christ, bearing record that Jesus is indeed the Son of God.

Our current culture tells us we have to put ourselves out there— be heard, be seen, be known. So many websites and apps cater to this mentality. Facebook, Twitter, Instagram, YouTube, Tumblr, the list goes on and on, and by the time you read this, those might be a thing of the past, replaced by something newer and better for self-promotion.

Let's be about Jesus-promotion instead. We can use those same platforms to point others to our Lord and Savior, not to ourselves. Let's let Him be heard, be seen, and be known to this world that is desperately in need of some light in the darkness.

Mark 1:16–20
Obey Me the First Time

As He was passing along by the Sea of Galilee, He saw Simon and Andrew, Simon's brother. They were casting a net into the sea, since they were fishermen.

"Follow Me," Jesus told them, "and I will make you fish for people!" Immediately they left their nets and followed Him. Going on a little farther, He saw James the son of Zebedee and his brother John. They were in their boat mending their nets. Immediately He called them, and they left their father Zebedee in the boat with the hired men and followed Him.

In an early learning center, the teachers help parents say to their children, "Obey me the first time." For example, when a parent asks a child to do a task, such as putting his shoes away, the parent says, "Go put away your shoes. Obey me the first time." Hearing this statement helps young children learn to respond respectfully to their parent's directive the first time the request is made. (The jury is still out on how well this method works, but it seems like it would be worth a try!)

Imagine for a moment what might have happened if Simon and Andrew had not obeyed Jesus the first time Jesus extended to them the invitation to follow Him. Not only would they have missed blessings in their own lives, they would have forfeited being a blessing to an infinite number of others—past, present, and future.

Contrast the disciples' story with that of the "rich man" we read about in Mark 10. He asked Jesus how one receives eternal life. The man said he had followed all the commandments in Scripture (which could be debatable), but he obviously knew something else was involved, or he wouldn't have asked Jesus the question. Jesus said to him, "You lack one thing: Go, sell all you have and give to the poor, and you will have treasure in heaven. Then come, follow Me." (Mark 10:21). Jesus told the man what he needed to do to follow Him. Did the man do it? No. Mark says the man "went away grieving, because he had many possessions" (v. 22). Just imagine! This man could have spent time with Jesus, but he didn't obey. Did he obey later? Perhaps. We would hope so. But even if he did, we know how short Jesus' time on earth was, and the rich man missed out because he didn't obey the first time.

As we seek direction from the Lord, are we ready, any time He calls, to obey Him the first time? Are we willing to do whatever He says, whenever He asks, for as long as He asks? He may not call us to give up our jobs and leave everything we know. He may not ask us to sell everything and give to the poor. But He might. Are we willing to deny ourselves and follow Him?

John 1:38–51
Come and See

When Jesus turned and noticed them following Him, He asked them, "What are you looking for?"

They said to Him, "Rabbi" (which means "Teacher"), "where are You staying?"

"Come and you'll see," He replied. So they went and saw where He was staying, and they stayed with Him that day. It was about 10 in the morning.

Andrew, Simon Peter's brother, was one of the two who heard John and followed Him. He first found his own brother Simon and told him, "We have found the Messiah!" (which means "Anointed One"), and he brought Simon to Jesus.

When Jesus saw him, He said, "You are Simon, son of John. You will be called Cephas" (which means "Rock").

The next day He decided to leave for Galilee. Jesus found Philip and told him, "Follow Me!"

Now Philip was from Bethsaida, the hometown of Andrew and Peter. Philip found Nathanael and told him, "We have found the One Moses wrote about in the Law (and so did the prophets): Jesus the son of Joseph, from Nazareth!"

"Can anything good come out of Nazareth?" Nathanael asked him.

"Come and see," Philip answered.

Then Jesus saw Nathanael coming toward Him and said about him, "Here is a true Israelite; no deceit is in him."

"How do you know me?" Nathanael asked.

"Before Philip called you, when you were under the fig tree, I saw you," Jesus answered.

"Rabbi," Nathanael replied, "You are the Son of God! You are the King of Israel!"

Jesus responded to him, "Do you believe only because I told you I saw you under the fig tree? You will see greater things than this." Then He said, "I assure you: You will see heaven opened and the angels of God ascending and descending on the Son of Man."

As Jesus began His ministry, one of His first tasks was to gather a group of followers who eventually became the apostles. Each calling was a bit unique. And in more than one case, one man told another about Him. Note that when Philip told Nathaniel that he had found the Messiah, Nathaniel was skeptical, because Jesus was from Nazareth. Nazareth did not have a good reputation. Instead of arguing with him, Philip simply said, "Come and see."

It is doubtful that anyone knows of a skeptic who became a Christian because someone else argued him into it. There is a difference between arguing with someone and leading them to see the truth of Christ through the claims of Scripture.

In a culture that is less Christian, we should become less argumentative with those who are skeptical of the claims of Christ, and consider inviting them to see what Christ has done and where He is currently at work.

Luke 5:1–11
Patiently Fish

As the crowd was pressing in on Jesus to hear God's word, He was standing by Lake Gennesaret. He saw two boats at the edge of the lake; the fishermen had left them and were washing their nets. He got into one of the boats, which belonged to Simon, and asked him to put out a little from the land. Then He sat down and was teaching the crowds from the boat.

When He had finished speaking, He said to Simon, "Put out into deep water and let down your nets for a catch."

"Master," Simon replied, "we've worked hard all night long and caught nothing! But at Your word, I'll let down the nets."

When they did this, they caught a great number of fish, and their nets began to tear. So they signaled to their partners in the other boat to come and help them; they came and filled both boats so full that they began to sink.

When Simon Peter saw this, he fell at Jesus' knees and said, "Go away from me, because I'm a sinful man, Lord!" For he and all those with him were amazed at the catch of fish they took, and so were James and John, Zebedee's sons, who were Simon's partners.

"Don't be afraid," Jesus told Simon. "From now on you will be catching people!" Then they brought the boats to land, left everything, and followed Him.

Fishing is sometimes discouraging. Wait, wait, and wait some more—then come up empty.

Peter was frustrated with his empty nets, as we all would be with a job that hadn't been accomplished. But when Peter saw how Jesus loaded them down with fish, he and his business partners were amazed to the point of abandoning their efforts and aligning themselves with Jesus' plan.

Peter, Andrew, James, and John were confronted with the ultimate life-changing moment: the call of Jesus. They were given a new life purpose. They no longer would be catching fish. They would be focused on something more important than that—bringing others to Jesus.

The call of the Lord brings change to us as well. We cannot return to our former way of life. Rather, we also are to give ourselves over to following Him and bringing others to Him.

Do you think the disciples ever got discouraged again? Yes, but they continued doing what Jesus told them to do. And the Lord brought "big catches" again—three thousand on the day of Pentecost alone.

When we get too weighed down with the emptiness of our nets, we must remember Jesus is the one who brings the catch. Whether we are witnessing to a stubborn friend or praying that a wayward child will come to Him, we are simply to patiently fish.

Luke 5:27–32
Who Needs the Doctor?

After this, Jesus went out and saw a tax collector named Levi sitting at the tax office, and He said to him, "Follow Me!" So, leaving everything behind, he got up and began to follow Him.

Then Levi hosted a grand banquet for Him at his house. Now there was a large crowd of tax collectors and others who were guests with them. But the Pharisees and their scribes were complaining to His disciples, "Why do you eat and drink with tax collectors and sinners?"

Jesus replied to them, "The healthy don't need a doctor, but the sick do. I have not come to call the righteous, but sinners to repentance."

A doctor has many patients. Some have serious diseases or conditions—cancer, multiple sclerosis, Parkinson's, Alzheimer's, lupus, AIDS. Others have minor problems—influenza, the common cold, a broken finger, a sinus infection. Some patients see the doctor every week; others see him once every three years. Some will see the doctor for no good reason at all, but most people don't go see the doctor unless they are sick. But at some point, everyone gets sick, and everyone needs a doctor.

Greek philosopher Epicurus (341–270 BC) called his teaching the "medicine of salvation." Another philosopher, Epictetus (AD 55–135), is said to have named his lecture room "the hospital for the sick soul." Sandwiched between the lives of these two mere wise men was Jesus Christ, the God-man, who delivered this ten-word parable: "The healthy don't need a doctor, but the sick do" (Luke 5:31). Who made up His questioners? A group of religious leaders more concerned with their own holiness than with helping others find forgiveness.

The Pharisees didn't realize why Jesus had come. He wasn't there to tell them how great they were; He was there to tell them they all had a sickness called sin, and He was the doctor who could fix it. Not only did they not see that He was there for the sick; they didn't realize that they were sick, too. After all, everyone gets sick; everyone needs a doctor at some time or another.

Jesus' few words to these men are packed with truth. They show Christ's great love for sinners. He didn't let tradition keep Him from bringing lost ones the hope of the gospel. He knew why He had come, and He let the Pharisees know they wouldn't stop Him from fulfilling His mission.

Are we like the Pharisees, who were quick to diagnose sin, but not the least bit concerned to help cure it (or to see it in themselves)? Or are we like Matthew, who hosted a party and invited his sin-sick friends to meet the Great Physician?

John 2:1–12
Jesus' First Miracle

On the third day a wedding took place in Cana of Galilee. Jesus' mother was there, and Jesus and His disciples were invited to the wedding as well. When the wine ran out, Jesus' mother told Him, "They don't have any wine."

"What has this concern of yours to do with Me, woman?" Jesus asked. "My hour has not yet come."

"Do whatever He tells you," His mother told the servants.

Now six stone water jars had been set there for Jewish purification. Each contained 20 or 30 gallons.

"Fill the jars with water," Jesus told them. So they filled them to the brim. Then He said to them, "Now draw some out and take it to the chief servant." And they did.

When the chief servant tasted the water (after it had become wine), he did not know where it came from—though the servants who had drawn the water knew. He called the groom and told him, "Everyone sets out the fine wine first, then, after people have drunk freely, the inferior. But you have kept the fine wine until now."

Jesus performed this first sign in Cana of Galilee. He displayed His glory, and His disciples believed in Him.

After this, He went down to Capernaum, together with His mother, His brothers, and His disciples, and they stayed there only a few days.

We might think that a wedding at noon, followed by an informal reception, then followed later by an evening dinner is a long wedding. But in Jesus' day, wedding celebrations could last a week. The groom was financially responsible for this extended party, and we know the guests were not just limited to family, since Jesus, His mother, and His disciples were all present. A wedding was quite a financial undertaking.

Added to the financial stress was the knowledge that running out of food or drink would bring great embarrassment to the family. This was just the situation Jesus found Himself in.

Mary saw the problem, and she informed Jesus. He responded in what might seem to be a rude fashion, but by using the word "woman," He was simply distancing Himself from her, for reasons that we can only speculate upon. Jesus wasn't ready to start revealing His power to the world, but His mother insisted, and He acquiesced.

We don't know exactly what Mary expected Jesus to do, but there was likely surprise from many, if not all, of the observers when they saw what He did—turn six large containers of water into wine, and not just any wine, but quality wine.

Not everyone knew where this wine had come from, but we can rest assured that those who knew were astonished by His power. We read that because of this display of His glory, His disciples believed in Him.

We, too, can believe in the power of Christ. He can and does work miracles, the most amazing of which is the miracle He does in our hearts when we choose to trust in Him.

John 3:1–8
You Must Be Born Again

There was a man from the Pharisees named Nicodemus, a ruler of the Jews. This man came to Him at night and said, "Rabbi, we know that You have come from God as a teacher, for no one could perform these signs You do unless God were with him."

Jesus replied, "I assure you: Unless someone is born again, he cannot see the kingdom of God."

"But how can anyone be born when he is old?" Nicodemus asked Him. "Can he enter his mother's womb a second time and be born?"

Jesus answered, "I assure you: Unless someone is born of water and the Spirit, he cannot enter the kingdom of God. Whatever is born of the flesh is flesh, and whatever is born of the Spirit is spirit. Do not be amazed that I told you that you must be born again. The wind blows where it pleases, and you hear its sound, but you don't know where it comes from or where it is going. So it is with everyone born of the Spirit."

Have you ever wondered what the phrase "born again" means? Nicodemus approached Jesus at night. He was curious about Jesus and the kingdom of God. Jesus told him he must be born again. Nicodemus was confused by this answer.

Nicodemus was a highly moral man who obeyed God's law. He was a respected leader of the Jewish community. No doubt he was a fine man. Yet something was lacking. Like Nicodemus, many people today confuse religion with new birth in Christ. Phrases like "I pray regularly" or "I believe there is a God" often are confused with a real new birth experience.

New birth begins with the Holy Spirit convicting a person that the person is a sinner. Because of sin, we are spiritually dead. For this reason, spiritual birth, as Jesus described it, is necessary. God loves us and gives us spiritual birth when we ask Him for it.

The Bible says all persons are sinners (Rom. 3:23). Jesus died on a cross and was raised from the dead to save sinners. To be born again means that a person admits to God that he or she is a sinner, repents of sin, believes in or trusts Christ, and confesses faith in Christ as Savior and Lord. Jesus told Nicodemus that everyone who believes in (places faith in) Christ would not perish (John 3:16). Jesus is the only One who can save us (John 14:6).

To believe in Jesus is to be born again. Confess your sins and ask Jesus right now to save you. "Then everyone who calls on the name of the Lord will be saved" (Acts 2:21). After you have received Jesus Christ into your life, share your decision with another person and follow Christ's example, then ask for baptism by immersion in a local Bible-believing church as a public expression of your faith (Rom. 6:4; Col. 2:6).

John 3:26–36
Jesus' Spokesperson

So they came to John and told him, "Rabbi, the One you testified about, and who was with you across the Jordan, is baptizing—and everyone is flocking to Him."

John responded, "No one can receive a single thing unless it's given to him from heaven. You yourselves can testify that I said, 'I am not the Messiah, but I've been sent ahead of Him.' He who has the bride is the groom. But the groom's friend, who stands by and listens for him, rejoices greatly at the groom's voice. So this joy of mine is complete. He must increase, but I must decrease."

The One who comes from above is above all. The one who is from the earth is earthly and speaks in earthly terms. The One who comes from heaven is above all. He testifies to what He has seen and heard, yet no one accepts His testimony. The one who has accepted His testimony has affirmed that God is true. For God sent Him, and He speaks God's words, since He gives the Spirit without measure. The Father loves the Son and has given all things into His hands. The one who believes in the Son has eternal life, but the one who refuses to believe in the Son will not see life; instead, the wrath of God remains on him.

In today's world, it's not unusual for a celebrity, an athlete, or a person of power to have a spokesperson who is authorized to speak on his or her behalf. The job of this person is to be the voice of someone else, to speak with authority and integrity. Perhaps the most visible of these spokespeople today is the White House Press Secretary. This person is tasked with telling the media—and through them the American people—the facts of what is happening in the world and the country, as well as the president and other senior government officials' reactions and plans regarding those situations. The press secretary doesn't speak for herself; she speaks for something bigger—the White House. Her job is to lift up the president, not herself.

John the Baptist had the unique and daunting assignment of the speaking for the Savior of the World. As the one who prepared the way for Jesus, John's role was to point people to the Messiah, the Son of God. In order to do his job effectively, John had to lift up someone other than himself—not an easy task for most humans.

In today's passage, John executed his job well. He declared that Jesus was sent from God the Father. Jesus spoke the very words of God. Everything God had and was and possessed, Jesus had and was and possessed. Jesus and the Father were and are one.

What a declaration! What a promise! What a Savior! And what an opportunity for those of us who call Him Lord to emulate. John was bold and unswerving in his proclamation of Jesus. Can we do any less?

John 4:1–15
Living Water

When Jesus knew that the Pharisees heard He was making and baptizing more disciples than John (though Jesus Himself was not baptizing, but His disciples were), He left Judea and went again to Galilee. He had to travel through Samaria, so He came to a town of Samaria called Sychar near the property that Jacob had given his son Joseph. Jacob's well was there, and Jesus, worn out from His journey, sat down at the well. It was about six in the evening.

A woman of Samaria came to draw water.

"Give Me a drink," Jesus said to her, for His disciples had gone into town to buy food.

"How is it that You, a Jew, ask for a drink from me, a Samaritan woman?" she asked Him. For Jews do not associate with Samaritans.

Jesus answered, "If you knew the gift of God, and who is saying to you, 'Give Me a drink,' you would ask Him, and He would give you living water."

"Sir," said the woman, "You don't even have a bucket, and the well is deep. So where do You get this 'living water'? You aren't greater than our father Jacob, are You? He gave us the well and drank from it himself, as did his sons and livestock."

Jesus said, "Everyone who drinks from this water will get thirsty again. But whoever drinks from the water that I will give him will never get thirsty again—ever! In fact, the water I will give him will become a well of water springing up within him for eternal life."

"Sir," the woman said to Him, "give me this water so I won't get thirsty and come here to draw water."

Lugging her empty water jar to the well in the midday heat must have been a tedious chore for the Samaritan woman. She was shocked when a Jewish man crossed a huge cultural barrier and asked her for a drink of water. Isn't it amazing that a simple request opened a window into the woman's dry, barren heart? Jesus knew her need—one deeper than a thirst for water.

As water is essential to our physical survival, Jesus' offer of living water is indispensable to our spiritual preservation. But we can't give away what we don't possess. If Christ's living presence isn't invigorating us, we have nothing to offer anyone else.

In looking around our neighborhood or workplace, do we see people through the eyes of Jesus? Are we prepared to show people His compassion when we see the signs of spiritual thirst and lostness? How can we connect with these individuals and engage them in conversation? Jesus left us this amazing model.

Or perhaps you're the one who's thirsty. Come, drink from His water and thirst no more!

John 4:46–53
The Man Believed

Then He went again to Cana of Galilee, where He had turned the water into wine. There was a certain royal official whose son was ill at Capernaum. When this man heard that Jesus had come from Judea into Galilee, he went to Him and pleaded with Him to come down and heal his son, for he was about to die.

Jesus told him, "Unless you people see signs and wonders, you will not believe."

"Sir," the official said to Him, "come down before my boy dies!"

"Go," Jesus told him, "your son will live." The man believed what Jesus said to him and departed.

While he was still going down, his slaves met him saying that his boy was alive. He asked them at what time he got better. "Yesterday at seven in the morning the fever left him," they answered. The father realized this was the very hour at which Jesus had told him, "Your son will live." Then he himself believed, along with his whole household.

G od has promised to take care of us," Jenna said to her husband. "It's right here in His Word, and He will do it in His own creative way," she continued. "We just have to trust Him." The past several months had been difficult, and Nathan's career and livelihood were on the line. Jenna and Nathan cried out to God in prayer that evening, believing the Lord would indeed work in their situation. Then they walked each day with the quiet confidence that God would fulfill His promise, in His time, in His way; and He did.

The nobleman in today's devotional passage faced a desperate situation. His son was dying, and he traveled a long way because he knew Jesus could heal him. The man believed that Jesus was the answer and trusted Him to work in His divine way in the circumstance. When Jesus said the man's son wouldn't die, the man fully believed Him, even though Jesus hadn't even seen the son. His belief was then justified when he discovered that his son was healed the moment Jesus had said the son would live.

Where do you stand today? Is there a circumstance in your life where you aren't trusting God, fully believing that He is the answer? Are you in despair over your spouse's medical problem, your child's wandering heart, your unemployment, a broken relationship? Trust God with it. Walk confidently, trusting that He is sovereign and at work in the midst of your circumstances.

Matthew 5:14–16
This Little Light

You are the light of the world. A city situated on a hill cannot be hidden. No one lights a lamp and puts it under a basket, but rather on a lampstand, and it gives light for all who are in the house. In the same way, let your light shine before men, so that they may see your good works and give glory to your Father in heaven.

The classic children's song "This Little Light of Mine" might seem infantile. It's short, and it doesn't have many words. It's fun for children to sing in the front of the church while holding up their pointer fingers. (And inevitably at least one of those fingers ends up in a nostril, adding to the hilarity.) But how often are the words explained to those little ones? Do we know what they're singing about or why it's sung at all? What light? Why does it shine? Why should it shine?

In this passage from Matthew's Gospel (a part of the Sermon on the Mount), Jesus was teaching His followers to live so that their lives lit up the darkness around them. When we are surrounded by darkness, it is amazing what just a little light does: it chases away the darkness. Think of how noticeable the light from one cell phone screen can be in a dark theater. Or consider how the power light on your laptop can turn a typically dark room into what seems like a light chamber.

Similarly, the presence of just one Christian in a group of people can completely change the tenor of a conversation. Certain questionable topics suddenly become off-limits. Others may think twice about the words they use. They may still say them, but at least they have considered the fact that maybe they shouldn't. Or think about how the actions of one Christian family serving others in their neighborhood can result in others wondering why they're doing it. This can lead to spiritual conversations, as well as a domino effect of people "paying it forward." Before you know it, neighbors are friends instead of mere acquaintances. They begin to spend time together instead of giving a quick wave before pulling into their garages and closing the door.

Hidden lights, like secret Christians, defeat their purpose. If we keep the light of our faith hidden, the darkness rules in our world. But when the world sees our light (His light in us), then the ways that we think, talk, and act will be a reflection of our Father. And many people will praise God when they see the light of our good works shining in the darkness.

Sing it together now: "This little light of mine, I'm gonna let it shine, let it shine, let it shine."

Matthew 5:38–48
Over-deliver

"You have heard that it was said, An eye for an eye and a tooth for a tooth. But I tell you, don't resist an evildoer. On the contrary, if anyone slaps you on your right cheek, turn the other to him also. As for the one who wants to sue you and take away your shirt, let him have your coat as well. And if anyone forces you to go one mile, go with him two. Give to the one who asks you, and don't turn away from the one who wants to borrow from you.

"You have heard that it was said, Love your neighbor and hate your enemy. But I tell you, love your enemies and pray for those who persecute you, so that you may be sons of your Father in heaven. For He causes His sun to rise on the evil and the good, and sends rain on the righteous and the unrighteous. For if you love those who love you, what reward will you have? Don't even the tax collectors do the same? And if you greet only your brothers, what are you doing out of the ordinary? Don't even the Gentiles do the same? Be perfect, therefore, as your heavenly Father is perfect.

U nder-promise. Over-deliver." This concept is often taught in the business world. It keeps expectations low, so when they're exceeded, the client thinks he or she has received something above and beyond. On the other hand, when the promises exceed the delivery, the client will be disappointed and expect a refund.

The scribes and Pharisees fell into the latter category. They were more about over-promising and under-delivering. They detailed the finer points of the Law without actually practicing what they preached. They had no problem flapping their gums for long periods of time about what was expected of others. Yet all of their words lacked one major component: the authority of a life with follow-through.

Do we, like the scribes, talk much but achieve little? We may promise to pray, but do we actually spend time on our knees? We talk about witnessing, yet do we follow through? We say it's important to have compassion on the poor, but do we actually do anything to help the poor in our communities? We post "Love your enemies" on social media, but do we show love to the coworker who took credit for our project? Such over-promising and under-delivering is a sad indictment on Christianity today.

A man of authority, Christ exemplified a life that didn't merely promise; He also delivered. He "walked the walk" without so much talk. If only we would talk a little less about spiritual things and just take the steps. To truly go the extra mile, may we be people who under-promise and yet over-deliver in all that we say and do.

Matthew 6:1–4
How to Give Well

Be careful not to practice your righteousness in front of people, to be seen by them. Otherwise, you will have no reward from your Father in heaven. So whenever you give to the poor, don't sound a trumpet before you, as the hypocrites do in the synagogues and on the streets, to be applauded by people. I assure you: They've got their reward! But when you give to the poor, don't let your left hand know what your right hand is doing, so that your giving may be in secret. And your Father who sees in secret will reward you.

One of the most difficult things in life is to be unnoticed. We want people to notice us, and this has never been more obvious than in this era of social media. How often do we post a picture of an amazing vacation spot, our kids doing something cute, or our trendy new living room design, hoping to get a bunch of "likes" and comments?

Barely a day goes by when we don't see an article in the news or a social media post about a celebrity who gave $20,000 to a charity or visited cancer patients in a children's hospital. We may roll our eyes, thinking that $20,000 to them is equal to $20 to us. Or we wonder if they're visiting those kids just for the photo op and publicity.

But don't we often do the same? Our small group serves a meal at a homeless shelter, and twenty pictures show up on Instagram. Or our child sets up a lemonade stand and gives the $5 earned to a charity, and we brag about it on our Facebook page. Or we see a stranger with a flat tire and stop to help, and we "live tweet" the entire experience.

We are not always looking for a parade in our honor but a digital "pat on the back" never hurts. Right? Wrong.

As Jesus taught on the life of faith, He reminded us that giving must be done simply for the sake of giving. When done for show, approval, or applause, it ruins the purpose. Rather than focusing on the one in need, we ask everyone to focus on us.

This passage in Matthew's Gospel is clear. We should be givers. In fact, our heavenly Father wants to reward us for doing so. Just as He looks after the poor and the outcast, so should His people. In this sermon from Jesus, He gives us the necessary guidance about how to do well at giving.

The key Jesus points to is to give quietly or, perhaps, even anonymously. As we mature in our faith, this kind of giving allows us to not be the center of attention. By growing up, we will place others before the Lord for their needs to be met.

As He makes use of us in the work, we find our full reward in our relationship with Him.

Matthew 6:5–8
Six Words

"Whenever you pray, you must not be like the hypo-crites, because they love to pray standing in the synagogues and on the street corners to be seen by people. I assure you: They've got their reward! But when you pray, go into your private room, shut your door, and pray to your Father who is in secret. And your Father who sees in secret will reward you. When you pray, don't babble like the idolaters, since they imagine they'll be heard for their many words. Don't be like them, because your Father knows the things you need before you ask Him.

"Therefore, you should pray like this: Our Father in heaven, Your name be honored as holy. Your kingdom come. Your will be done on earth as it is in heaven. Give us today our daily bread. And forgive us our debts, as we also have forgiven our debtors. And do not bring us into temptation, but deliver us from the evil one. [For Yours is the king-dom and the power and the glory forever. Amen.]"

Jesus told His disciples that long, flowery prayers do not make the Father listen any closer or answer any faster. God already knows what we need before we even ask. The exact words we say will deter-mine whether He will answer our prayers in the way we want. There is no formula that says, "If you pray in this order, using a certain amount of words, then God is more likely to answer." Most who are reading this would find that thought absurd and agree that it sounds silly.

However, have you ever prayed with the wrong motive? Have you ever prayed and tried to "guilt" God into answering? Have you ever prayed and tried to sound humble so the Lord would be more likely to answer?

Jesus called out those who prayed in public for others to see and admire. A modern-day example of this might be the prayer time in small group Bible studies. Evaluate whether you choose to pray out loud in these groups to impress others in the study or to really talk to the Lord.

Instead of praying in those ways, Jesus says, "You should pray like this" (v. 9). What's striking about this model prayer is verse 11: "Give us today our daily bread." Only six out of the sixty-nine words of this prayer are focused on our own needs. That's 9 percent. The other 91 percent deals with other issues far more important, such as the glory of God and His kingdom, the manifestation of His will, the mandate of forgiveness, and the responsibility of denying sin and relying upon His power. This is important stuff.

How do our own prayers stack up, percentage-wise? Do we spend an inordinate percentage of our prayer time asking God for things for ourselves? We already know that the length of our prayers is not important. But the basic content of our prayers is. Let's commit to focusing less on our own needs in prayer and focus on the one who fills those needs, often without us even asking.

Matthew 6:24–34
The Remedy for Anxiety

No one can be a slave of two masters, since either he will hate one and love the other, or be devoted to one and despise the other. You cannot be slaves of God and of money.

This is why I tell you: Don't worry about your life, what you will eat or what you will drink; or about your body, what you will wear. Isn't life more than food and the body more than clothing? Look at the birds of the sky: They don't sow or reap or gather into barns, yet your heavenly Father feeds them. Aren't you worth more than they? Can any of you add a single cubit to his height by worrying? And why do you worry about clothes? Learn how the wildflowers of the field grow: they don't labor or spin thread. Yet I tell you that not even Solomon in all his splendor was adorned like one of these! If that's how God clothes the grass of the field, which is here today and thrown into the furnace tomorrow, won't He do much more for you—you of little faith? So don't worry, saying, "What will we eat?" or "What will we drink?" or "What will we wear?" For the idolaters eagerly seek all these things, and your heavenly Father knows that you need them. But seek first the kingdom of God and His righteousness, and all these things will be provided for you. Therefore don't worry about tomorrow, because

*tomorrow will worry about itself. Each day has
enough trouble of its own.*

Living above worry is much easier said than done. Our most basic
needs—what we eat, what we drink, and what we wear—are
indeed recurring needs. There is never a day that we do not need them.

Many reading this do not often worry about whether we'll have
enough money to put food on the table or clothe our families. But we
still worry about being able to afford the things we don't really need—a
bigger house, a college education for our children, the latest technological gadget, more clothes. These things all too often absorb much of our
time, thought, and emotional energy.

In the Sermon on the Mount, Jesus challenges our natural inclinations: "Don't collect for yourselves treasures on earth" (Matt. 6:19),
"You cannot be slaves of God and of money" (v. 24), do not obsess over
your daily needs (see v. 31). These are many of the things that keep us
earth-focused instead of God-centered.

In contrast, Jesus offers two challenging alternatives. "But collect
for yourselves treasures in heaven . . ." (v. 20). "But seek first the kingdom of God and His righteousness . . ." (v. 33).

In effect, Jesus said, "If you do this (seek Me first), then I will
provide that (the things you are prone to worry about)." We will find
that when we seek Him, He will provide the things we need, so we have
no reason to be anxious.

Matthew 7:1–5
Acknowledge the Log

Do not judge, so that you won't be judged. For with the judgment you use, you will be judged, and with the measure you use, it will be measured to you. Why do you look at the speck in your brother's eye but don't notice the log in your own eye? Or how can you say to your brother, "Let me take the speck out of your eye," and look, there's a log in your eye? Hypocrite! First take the log out of your eye, and then you will see clearly to take the speck out of your brother's eye.

B eginning the Sermon on the Mount (Matt. 5:1—7:29) with the Beatitudes and ending with the parable of the wise man who built his house on a rock, Jesus taught with authority. From beginning to end, this sermon is packed with simple, yet hard-to-live truths, one of which is the command not to judge and thereby become a hypocrite.

Have you ever been guilty of being a hypocrite? Once, while driving, a father expounded eloquently to his young daughters about how a very influential state politician had lied about his education. All agreeing that it was very wrong, they drove a short distance in silence. Then one of the daughters asked, "Dad, wouldn't it also be lying to tell people we caught more fish than we really did?" The father couldn't deny it. He had also been guilty of hypocrisy.

The previous verses paint a compelling visual of what hypocrisy looks like. Can't you just imagine cartoon characters playing the parts of the two men? There's one guy with a little speck of dust in his eye. He's blinking hard and maybe even rubbing his eye. Then there's the man with a tree trunk protruding out of his eye without even noticing it. He just goes walking around, knocking people down with that huge log but pointing out the speck of dust in the other guy's eye. One wonders how he could even get close enough to notice that speck without doing damage to the other man. The truth is, he can't. First, he has to acknowledge that he has a log, and then he has to remove it. Only then can he truly help the man with the speck.

Jesus made it plain enough, even for children, that while we may have different levels of accountability among family, friends, countrymen, and enemies, God has only one standard for us all: "Be perfect, therefore, as your heavenly Father is perfect" (Matt. 5:48).

Let's strive to be self-aware enough to realize when we have a log in our eye. In fact, let's also be cognizant of our own specks, and ask Jesus to remove them. Then we can not only properly see others' specks, but we can also tell them from experience how they can be removed—only through the power of Jesus.

Matthew 7:15–23
Fruit Inspectors

Beware of false prophets who come to you in sheep's clothing but inwardly are ravaging wolves. You'll recognize them by their fruit. Are grapes gathered from thornbushes or figs from thistles? In the same way, every good tree produces good fruit, but a bad tree produces bad fruit. A good tree can't produce bad fruit; neither can a bad tree produce good fruit. Every tree that doesn't produce good fruit is cut down and thrown into the fire. So you'll recognize them by their fruit.

"Not everyone who says to Me, "Lord, Lord!" will enter the kingdom of heaven, but only the one who does the will of My Father in heaven. On that day many will say to Me, "Lord, Lord, didn't we prophesy in Your name, drive out demons in Your name, and do many miracles in Your name?" Then I will announce to them, "I never knew you! Depart from Me, you lawbreakers!"

We live in an age where anyone with a keyboard, a smart phone, or a webcam can have a voice in our culture. If you can turn a clever phrase and state your opinion well, you become an "expert." But these so-called experts who are spouting suppositions instead of facts will quickly send their consumers off course if they are not the real deal.

This is not a new problem. Satan is the father of lies and has had mouthpieces aplenty throughout history. God's people have always had to be on guard against wolves in sheep's clothing, and in the digital age with information so readily available, this has never been truer. One Internet search of a biblical topic can easily yield tens of thousands of results. How do we know which voices to listen to? At first glance, it can be difficult to determine who the real experts are.

The same can be true in nature. Looking at trees, it can be hard to identify them. Their bark and leaves are similar, and at times, until you see fruit, they can be hard to differentiate. That is what Jesus is conveying here. Some of those who claim to be believers and/or theological experts may actually be tools of the great deceiver himself.

A false prophet can look like the real thing until you examine the fruit of his life. How does he live? Does his life consistently line up with biblical truth? Do the doctrines he's teaching line up with God's revealed Word? If anything does not match up with Truth, we need to throw it out.

Scripture says, "Dear friends, do not believe every spirit, but test the spirits to determine if they are from God, because many false prophets have gone out into the world" (1 John 4:1). The battle is for our minds, and we must be vigilant fruit inspectors if we are to gain the victory.

Matthew 7:24–29
A Strong Foundation

"Therefore, everyone who hears these words of Mine and acts on them will be like a sensible man who built his house on the rock. The rain fell, the rivers rose, and the winds blew and pounded that house. Yet it didn't collapse, because its foundation was on the rock. But everyone who hears these words of Mine and doesn't act on them will be like a foolish man who built his house on the sand. The rain fell, the rivers rose, the winds blew and pounded that house, and it collapsed. And its collapse was great!"

When Jesus had finished this sermon, the crowds were astonished at His teaching, because He was teaching them like one who had authority, and not like their scribes.

Small, eager hands pack damp sand into a pail and dump it out on the beach. Over and over again—pack and dump. Higher and higher the sand castle grows. Impressive towers delight the eyes until the child sees the incoming nibble at the shoreline. Frothy waves lick the strands of kelp, then drain back into the sea. Another wave swishes away footprints of beach combers. Quick! Dig the moat deeper. Protect the castle!

A watchful father swoops his anxious child into his arms, lifting him high as a wave reaches the edge of the castle and fills the moat.

The next wave comes in. None of the waves crash over the castle, but as the two watch, the castle slowly falls in upon itself. Its foundation of sand does not hold up against the water.

We all know that sand is not a great foundation to build anything on. Yet we often try to do it. Many of us have a tendency to trust in anything and everything to hold us up before we turn to the solidity of Christ.

When we put our faith in Jesus and seek to follow His commands, we're building our lives on a firm foundation that will not fail. It will not wash away with the waves, and it will not give in to the winds and storms that come along. Notice that Jesus doesn't say that storms will never come. He does promise that when we build our lives on Him, we have an unshakable foundation we can always count on.

We all face an uncertain world. People we love get sick and sometimes die. We, too, get sick. Disappointments come, arguments occur, and relationships are broken. But when we place our trust in Jesus, we can weather any storm based on His sure foundation.

Mark 2:1-12
More Than Physical Healing

When He entered Capernaum again after some days, it was reported that He was at home. So many people gathered together that there was no more room, not even in the doorway, and He was speaking the message to them. Then they came to Him bringing a paralytic, carried by four men. Since they were not able to bring him to Jesus because of the crowd, they removed the roof above where He was. And when they had broken through, they lowered the mat on which the paralytic was lying.

Seeing their faith, Jesus told the paralytic, "Son, your sins are forgiven."

But some of the scribes were sitting there, thinking to themselves: "Why does He speak like this? He's blaspheming! Who can forgive sins but God alone?"

Right away Jesus understood in His spirit that they were thinking like this within themselves and said to them, "Why are you thinking these things in your hearts? Which is easier: to say to the paralytic, 'Your sins are forgiven,' or to say, 'Get up, pick up your mat, and walk'? But so you may know that the Son of Man has authority on earth to forgive sins," *He told the paralytic, "I tell you: get up, pick up your mat, and go home."*

Immediately he got up, picked up the mat, and went out in front of everyone. As a result, they were all astounded and gave glory to God, saying, "We have never seen anything like this!"

I magine you have a brain tumor. The surgeon operates, and when you wake up after the procedure the doctor says, "Great news! I got all of the tumor, and I increased your IQ by 30 points while I was in there!" That would sound crazy, right? A doctor can't make you smarter.

The Pharisees may have had a similar response to Jesus when He declared that He had forgiven the paralyzed man's sins. First of all, a human can't forgive sin. And second—and more important to the Pharisees—the claim would be blasphemous. Only God can forgive sins, so this man was claiming to be God, which was a sin punishable by death.

Jesus knew what they were thinking, so He headed them off at the pass. The forgiveness of sins wasn't something that could be verified, but healing a paralytic was definitely verifiable. So He healed the man in order to show His authority and power.

He also shows us through this passage that He does have the power and authority to forgive sins. He forgave the paralytic's sins, and He can forgive ours. When we come to Him in faith, like the paralytic did, we can be sure that He will forgive our sins.

Luke 5:12–16

Rest in Him

While He was in one of the towns, a man was there who had a serious skin disease all over him. He saw Jesus, fell facedown, and begged Him: "Lord, if You are willing, You can make me clean."

Reaching out His hand, He touched him, saying, "I am willing; be made clean," and immediately the disease left him. Then He ordered him to tell no one: "But go and show yourself to the priest, and offer what Moses prescribed for your cleansing as a testimony to them."

But the news about Him spread even more, and large crowds would come together to hear Him and to be healed of their sicknesses. Yet He often withdrew to deserted places and prayed.

Quick! What time is it? Isn't there something else you should be doing right now? The kids need breakfast. You need to hit that deadline for work. Your wife just told you to mow the lawn before the neighbors report you to the HOA. The church called and they need a last-minute fill-in for a speaker at the men's banquet tonight. Your mom really needs you to check her credit card account balance online. The homeless shelter needs more volunteers for lunch today. A friend asked you to babysit so she and her husband can go out for a long-overdue date night. Your boss really needs you on-site for a meeting today.

We live in a busy society—one that leads us to act as if everything is a must-do. We must accept just one more responsibility at work, volunteer at just one more organization, and participate in just one more activity at church. We are rushed beyond measure to get everything done and keep everyone happy.

Think about this: Jesus was busy, but He was never rushed. He had only thirty-three years to accomplish more than we ever will (and only three of those years were spent in full-time ministry), but He always had time to be still, to wait patiently on His Father's timing, and to pray.

Although He was so tuned in to those around Him that He never missed an opportunity to minister, He did so without burnout, without total exhaustion. Jesus listened to God's marching orders and not to those of family, friends, or synagogue leaders.

No one understands, listens, or loves like God. Instead of competing for our time, He wants us to draw near to Him and be still so that we may hear His voice and follow Him.

Take some time right now to withdraw from the demands of the world and rest in Him.

John 8:30-41
The Truth Will Set You Free

As He was saying these things, many believed in Him. So Jesus said to the Jews who had believed Him, "If you continue in My word, you really are My disciples. You will know the truth, and the truth will set you free."

"We are descendants of Abraham," they answered Him, "and we have never been enslaved to anyone. How can You say, 'You will become free'?"

Jesus responded, "I assure you: Everyone who commits sin is a slave of sin. A slave does not remain in the household forever, but a son does remain forever. Therefore, if the Son sets you free, you really will be free. I know you are descendants of Abraham, but you are trying to kill Me because My word is not welcome among you. I speak what I have seen in the presence of the Father; therefore, you do what you have heard from your father."

"Our father is Abraham!" they replied.

"If you were Abraham's children," Jesus told them, "you would do what Abraham did. But now you are trying to kill Me, a man who has told you the truth that I heard from God. Abraham did not do this! You're doing what your father does."

It is no easy task to give freedom to someone who believes he already has it. Jesus offered freedom to the Jews, but in their minds they were already free because they were Abraham's descendants. They just could not get past that point. Being Abraham's children was all they needed, in their minds. To them, their status constituted freedom, but they missed the truth that Jesus pointed out: "Everyone who commits sin is a slave of sin" (John 8:34). If sin is someone's master, no status can constitute genuine freedom. Perceived freedom, if not based in absolute truth, is a delusion.

In nations where freedom is severely limited, citizens may be taught to believe they are free and may accept that as fact, until they see the freedoms experienced in other freer nations. In those freer nations, people believe their freedoms are absolute until certain laws encroach on their freedoms. But even when something better—and freer—is offered, people don't always want to accept it. Perhaps they think they can't really get it, but sometimes they simply think they don't need it— what they have is good enough. But those people who have the freedom the others reject know that it is so much better.

When it all comes down, only one freedom is absolute: the kind Jesus offered to those He addressed—not based on perceived status, but built on the spiritual status He provides through a personal relationship with Him. If you want to be really free, You must know Him, the Truth, in a relationship by grace through faith.

John 9:25-41
Was Blind but Now I See

He answered, "Whether or not He's a sinner, I don't know. One thing I do know: I was blind, and now I can see!"

Then they asked him, "What did He do to you? How did He open your eyes?"

"I already told you," he said, "and you didn't listen. Why do you want to hear it again? You don't want to become His disciples too, do you?"

They ridiculed him: "You're that man's disciple, but we're Moses' disciples. We know that God has spoken to Moses. But this man—we don't know where He's from!"

"This is an amazing thing," the man told them. "You don't know where He is from, yet He opened my eyes! We know that God doesn't listen to sinners, but if anyone is God-fearing and does His will, He listens to him. Throughout history no one has ever heard of someone opening the eyes of a person born blind. If this man were not from God, He wouldn't be able to do anything."

"You were born entirely in sin," they replied, "and are you trying to teach us?" Then they threw him out.

When Jesus heard that they had thrown the man out, He found him and asked, "Do you believe in the Son of Man?"

"Who is He, Sir, that I may believe in Him?" he asked.

Jesus answered, "You have seen Him; in fact, He is the One speaking with you."

"I believe, Lord!" he said, and he worshiped Him.

Jesus said, "I came into this world for judgment, in order that those who do not see will see and those who do see will become blind."

Some of the Pharisees who were with Him heard these things and asked Him, "We aren't blind too, are we?"

"If you were blind," Jesus told them, "you wouldn't have sin. But now that you say, 'We see'— your sin remains."

D o you remember what it was like the first time you balanced and pedaled a bicycle at the same time? What had seemed impossible all of a sudden made sense. Remember in third grade when the lights came on and suddenly the multiplication tables did not look like a foreign language? Have there been times when you were working on a project that wouldn't come together? Perhaps in frustration you closed you eyes, regulated your breathing, and counted to ten; and in your darkness the lights came on.

These experiences give us insight into what happens when Jesus enters the scene. He comes to bring judgment upon all that is untrue and unclear. When He enters, those who had been blind suddenly see and those who thought they could see find themselves in darkness without His light. The Light of the World illuminates those who seek Him in darkness and blinds those whose spiritual eyes have played tricks on them.

Thank God today for opening your eyes to the Light of Jesus. Or, if you are still living in darkness, ask the Light of the World to open your eyes.

Mark 5:25–34
Reach Out in Faith

A woman suffering from bleeding for 12 years had endured much under many doctors. She had spent everything she had and was not helped at all. On the contrary, she became worse. Having heard about Jesus, she came behind Him in the crowd and touched His robe. For she said, "If I can just touch His robes, I'll be made well!" Instantly her flow of blood ceased, and she sensed in her body that she was cured of her affliction.

At once Jesus realized in Himself that power had gone out from Him. He turned around in the crowd and said, "Who touched My robes?"

His disciples said to Him, "You see the crowd pressing against You, and You say, 'Who touched Me?'"

So He was looking around to see who had done this. Then the woman, knowing what had happened to her, came with fear and trembling, fell down before Him, and told Him the whole truth. "Daughter," He said to her, "your faith has made you well. Go in peace and be free from your affliction."

I n a way, this scene is reminiscent of current-day fans flocking around celebrities, just trying to catch a glimpse of her or touch the sleeve of his shirt. They want a brief brush with fame. Their goal is to take a selfie and have a good story to tell their friends and digital connections.

In the passage above, crowds were pressing around Jesus. Many of them would have been there because of his fame. But others were there for more. They had heard that He could cast out demons, make blind people see, and heal the lame. They wanted a little of that for themselves. That's why the woman was there.

We don't know the cause of the woman's issue of blood, but anyone can imagine how debilitating that would be. Twelve years of nonstop bleeding was not just an inconvenience. It also meant that she was constantly ceremonially unclean—as was anyone who touched anything she sat or lay on during those years. If she had been married, her husband had likely divorced her. She couldn't participate in religious ceremonies. She was essentially an outcast. Others wouldn't want to be around her for fear that they'd become unclean too.

Crowds huddled close together as this suffering woman saw Jesus pass by. Her money and doctors had failed her; she was worse off than ever before. She came behind the Lord and touched His garment, longing to be made whole, hoping that this was what Jesus would do.

When Jesus passed through the crowds that day, He'd begun to be noticed and sought out. But He was looking for faith, rather than those attracted to fame. This woman brought her physical needs to the only One who could truly help. And the Lord chose to heal her. She was able to go in peace, having been made whole.

When we are broken, tired, wounded, utterly spent—perhaps worse off than we've ever been—we, too, can purposefully come to Jesus. We draw close to Him in faith, knowing that He is able to meet all our needs.

John 6:24-36
Never Hunger or Thirst

When the crowd saw that neither Jesus nor His disciples were there, they got into the boats and went to Capernaum looking for Jesus.

When they found Him on the other side of the sea, they said to Him, "Rabbi, when did You get here?"

Jesus answered, "I assure you: You are looking for Me, not because you saw the signs, but because you ate the loaves and were filled. Don't work for the food that perishes but for the food that lasts for eternal life, which the Son of Man will give you, because God the Father has set His seal of approval on Him."

"What can we do to perform the works of God?" they asked.

Jesus replied, "This is the work of God—that you believe in the One He has sent."

"What sign then are You going to do so we may see and believe You?" they asked. "What are You going to perform? Our fathers ate the manna in the wilderness, just as it is written: He gave them bread from heaven to eat."

Jesus said to them, "I assure you: Moses didn't give you the bread from heaven, but My Father gives you the real bread from heaven. For the

bread of God is the One who comes down from
heaven and gives life to the world."

Then they said, "Sir, give us this bread always!"

"I am the bread of life," Jesus told them. "No
one who comes to Me will ever be hungry, and no
one who believes in Me will ever be thirsty again.
But as I told you, you've seen Me, and yet you do
not believe."

During World War II, Dr. Harry Coover was trying to develop a better gun sight for the Army. In the process, he created an incredibly strong glue. It wasn't what he was looking for, so he discarded it. Years later, while working on plastics for jet canopies, he came up with the sticky substance again. This time, he realized the importance of what we now call Super Glue.

In John 6 the people who sought out the Savior were expecting something different than He was offering. They wanted another free meal. He'd fed them from five loaves of bread and two fish the day before. But Jesus offered them something much better and more satisfying than earthly food; He offered the bread of life. All He required was simple belief in Him as the Son of God, but many ignored Him because they were looking for something else. He was offering them Himself.

Jesus still extends this offer to all who come to Him. The things of this world leave us unfulfilled and wanting more. He gives satisfaction and fulfills our longings. Only Jesus can keep our souls from hunger and thirst for eternity.

Luke 19:12–26
Well Done!

Therefore He said: "A nobleman traveled to a far country to receive for himself authority to be king and then return. He called 10 of his slaves, gave them 10 minas, and told them, 'Engage in business until I come back.'

"But his subjects hated him and sent a delegation after him, saying, 'We don't want this man to rule over us!'

"At his return, having received the authority to be king, he summoned those slaves he had given the money to, so he could find out how much they had made in business. The first came forward and said, 'Master, your mina has earned 10 more minas.'

"'Well done, good slave!' he told him. 'Because you have been faithful in a very small matter, have authority over 10 towns.'

"The second came and said, 'Master, your mina has made five minas.'

"So he said to him, 'You will be over five towns.'

"And another came and said, 'Master, here is your mina. I have kept it hidden away in a cloth because I was afraid of you, for you're a tough man: you collect what you didn't deposit and reap what you didn't sow.'

"He told him, 'I will judge you by what you have said, you evil slave! If you knew I was a tough

*man, collecting what I didn't deposit and reaping
what I didn't sow, why didn't you put my money in
the bank? And when I returned, I would have col-
lected it with interest!' So he said to those standing
there, 'Take the mina away from him and give it to
the one who has 10 minas.'*

"But they said to him, 'Master, he has 10 minas.'

*"'I tell you, that to everyone who has, more will
be given; and from the one who does not have,
even what he does have will be taken away.'"*

Today's devotional passage is akin to a similar passage in Matthew 25:14–30 that refers to talents. Those of us who have attended church from our childhood to adulthood have heard many a sermon and Sunday school lesson using these Scripture references as the focal point. Stewardship is the theme of both passages. Stewardship is about being accountable not only for our money, but for time and abilities with which God has gifted His children to use for His work.

Christians fall somewhere on a line between the extremes of being outstanding stewards and being totally irresponsible with God's gifts. Where are you in relation to these two extremes? Hopefully you will hear words similar to those heard by the first servant in Jesus' parable: "You have done well with what I have given you. Therefore, I am going to increase your responsibility and allow you to enjoy the fulfillment that goes along with those responsibilities." If you need to be a better steward of what God has given you, take some time right now to ask Him to help you use those gifts and resources in ways that will delight and honor Him.

Matthew 8:1-4
An Individual in the Multitude

When He came down from the mountain, large crowds followed Him. Right away a man with a serious skin disease came up and knelt before Him, saying, "Lord, if You are willing, You can make me clean."

Reaching out His hand He touched him, saying, "I am willing; be made clean." Immediately his disease was healed. Then Jesus told him, "See that you don't tell anyone; but go, show yourself to the priest, and offer the gift that Moses prescribed, as a testimony to them."

We all want to be singled out from among the crowd sometimes. We want to know that we are special and known by someone. Even if we are shy or have reserved personalities, still we desire to be important or significant to someone. We want someone to notice us.

After Jesus finished His Sermon on the Mount, the Bible says that multitudes followed Him. We cannot know exactly how many people this was, but it would have been a very large crowd, large enough for the individual to feel insignificant. Could Jesus know or care about just one?

The answer in Matthew 8:3 is a resounding yes! This passage moves us from the multitudes crowding in on Jesus to the individual. From the midst of the masses, one man came to Jesus for healing. Jesus stretched out His hand and touched him. The man was healed physically, but no doubt he was also healed emotionally and spiritually. Jesus knew about this leper's plight, and He knew about each individual following Him in that multitude. He knows about you, and He knows about me.

This picture is a powerful reminder. No matter how big the world, Jesus will always see you in the crowd. Jesus is a personal Savior. He died for a world of lost sinners, yet He remains your personal Redeemer. He never overlooks the least of us. He notices each dilemma you face. You will not get lost in the crowd.

The leper came and knelt before Jesus and he had Jesus' full attention. We, even from among a multitude, as we come and kneel before the Lord, have His full attention, too.

What healing or cleansing do you desire? Remember, Jesus knows you by name and feels every hurt you experience. Like the leper, you can say, "Lord, if You are willing, You can make me clean." Look up so you won't miss His powerful hand reaching down to touch you.

John 8:2–11
A Response to Sin

At dawn He went to the temple complex again, and all the people were coming to Him. He sat down and began to teach them.

Then the scribes and the Pharisees brought a woman caught in adultery, making her stand in the center. "Teacher," they said to Him, "this woman was caught in the act of committing adultery. In the law Moses commanded us to stone such women. So what do You say?" They asked this to trap Him, in order that they might have evidence to accuse Him.

Jesus stooped down and started writing on the ground with His finger. When they persisted in questioning Him, He stood up and said to them, "The one without sin among you should be the first to throw a stone at her."

Then He stooped down again and continued writing on the ground. When they heard this, they left one by one, starting with the older men. Only He was left, with the woman in the center. When Jesus stood up, He said to her, "Woman, where are they? Has no one condemned you?"

"No one, Lord," she answered.

"Neither do I condemn you," said Jesus. "Go, and from now on do not sin anymore."

When Martin was a young man, he could not understand why parents had so much trouble with their teenagers. As a high school counselor, he had been trained in behavior modification techniques. He believed that parents, with sufficient training, could effectively guide (or control) their older children.

Recently, with a teenager of his own, Martin discovered that it's not so simple. Even with a Christian upbringing (and behavior modification), young people can make poor choices, causing parents—and others—to wonder what they did wrong. Today, Martin is much less judgmental toward others. He says, "No one knows exactly what another person is going through."

In today's devotional passage, no one was qualified to judge the woman. The Pharisees all had sinned, and therefore they had no right to judge her. Only Jesus had that right, yet He didn't condemn her either. Instead of punishing her, He sent her on her way and told her to stop sinning.

Some people use this passage to say that Jesus was light on sin or that we have no right to call others out on their sin. But that's not what this passage communicates. We know from the rest of Jesus' ministry that He was not light on sin. And He pointed out people's sin quite often—especially the sins of those who acted as if they had none. That's what He was doing here. The Pharisees were being legalistic and hardhearted toward this woman, but He had mercy upon her. Likewise, our response to sin should never be that of humiliation and punishment but that of grace, mercy, and the desire to see the person turn from his or her sin.

Matthew 18:21–35

Forgive, as You Have Been Forgiven

Then Peter came to Him and said, "Lord, how many times could my brother sin against me and I forgive him? As many as seven times?"

"I tell you, not as many as seven," Jesus said to him, "but 70 times seven. For this reason, the kingdom of heaven can be compared to a king who wanted to settle accounts with his slaves. When he began to settle accounts, one who owed 10,000 talents was brought before him. Since he had no way to pay it back, his master commanded that he, his wife, his children, and everything he had be sold to pay the debt.

"At this, the slave fell facedown before him and said, 'Be patient with me, and I will pay you everything!' Then the master of that slave had compassion, released him, and forgave him the loan.

"But that slave went out and found one of his fellow slaves who owed him 100 denarii. He grabbed him, started choking him, and said, 'Pay what you owe!'

"At this, his fellow slave fell down and began begging him, 'Be patient with me, and I will pay you back.' But he wasn't willing. On the contrary, he went and threw him into prison until he could pay what was owed. When the other slaves saw what

had taken place, they were deeply distressed and went and reported to their master everything that had happened.

"Then, after he had summoned him, his master said to him, 'You wicked slave! I forgave you all that debt because you begged me. Shouldn't you also have had mercy on your fellow slave, as I had mercy on you?' And his master got angry and handed him over to the jailers to be tortured until he could pay everything that was owed. So My heavenly Father will also do to you if each of you does not forgive his brother from his heart."

The religious leaders in Jesus' day taught that while we should at first forgive people, there should be a limit on it. They set the bar at three times, so Peter likely thought he was being generous with seven. But Jesus dispensed with that notion very quickly. We should forgive seventy-times-seven times. Before you do the math on that, just know that Jesus wasn't really giving a limit. He was essentially saying: forgive as many times as you have the opportunity to do so.

The following parable makes clear why we should forgive. Like the slave was expected to forgive a debt because his owner had forgiven him for one, we should forgive others because God forgives us.

It's really that simple. But it's not always easy, is it? When you find it hard to forgive someone, take some time to remember all the things God has forgiven you for. You may then find it a little bit easier to show mercy to the other person and forgive just as God has forgiven you.

John 10:1–5
The Shepherd's Voice

"I assure you: Anyone who doesn't enter the sheep pen by the door but climbs in some other way, is a thief and a robber. The one who enters by the door is the shepherd of the sheep. The door-keeper opens it for him, and the sheep hear his voice. He calls his own sheep by name and leads them out. When he has brought all his own outside, he goes ahead of them. The sheep follow him because they recognize his voice. They will never follow a stranger; instead they will run away from him, because they don't recognize the voice of strangers."

The Holy Land tour group hesitated briefly beside a narrow road that wound through the desert. A young Bedouin shepherd was leading his flock of sheep toward a stand of small trees that indicated the possibility of a nearby stream of water. He was singing, probably an Arabic tune, when he noticed a couple of the sheep wandering from the others.

He cupped his hands to his mouth and began to sing louder. The animals stopped and turned back toward the shepherd. They knew his voice. Some eastern shepherds even call their sheep by name.

We can imagine that Jesus would have encountered similar scenes, though two millennia earlier. He was well acquainted with the work of shepherds, and the Pharisees must have been aware of it as well. Thus, while addressing the Pharisees who challenged Him, Jesus responded with a parable about sheep. The shepherds would keep their sheep in large enclosures that could be big enough for as many as a thousand sheep. The shepherds would enter the enclosure through a door, while thieves would try by other means to enter the sheepfold in order to steal. The sheep would become agitated by this intrusion. Only the shepherd's voice could give them security; it was the shepherd's voice that they would obey and follow.

Today's false shepherds attempt to lure and steal Jesus' followers away from Him. They discount the Shepherd's authority, sowing seeds of doubt. By appealing to our wish for power, selfish desires, and material gain, they pull us away. If we know Jesus' voice, however, we can rest in the security of His soothing presence and protection.

As our Shepherd, God—through the presence of His Holy Spirit who indwells us—assures us that we are uniquely His own sheep. We can know His voice. And He not only knows our names but also knows all about us. What a marvelous, personal sense of security we find in this awareness that we belong to Him.

Matthew 9:2–13
Mercy, not Sacrifice

Just then some men brought to Him a paralytic lying on a mat. Seeing their faith, Jesus told the paralytic, "Have courage, son, your sins are forgiven."

At this, some of the scribes said among themselves, "He's blaspheming!"

But perceiving their thoughts, Jesus said, "Why are you thinking evil things in your hearts? For which is easier: to say, 'Your sins are forgiven,' or to say, 'Get up and walk'? But so you may know that the Son of Man has authority on earth to forgive sins"—then He told the paralytic, "Get up, pick up your mat, and go home." And he got up and went home. When the crowds saw this, they were awestruck and gave glory to God who had given such authority to men.

As Jesus went on from there, He saw a man named Matthew sitting at the tax office, and He said to him, "Follow Me!" So he got up and followed Him.

While He was reclining at the table in the house, many tax collectors and sinners came as guests to eat with Jesus and His disciples. When the Pharisees saw this, they asked His disciples, "Why does your Teacher eat with tax collectors and sinners?"

> *But when He heard this, He said, "Those who are well don't need a doctor, but the sick do. Go and learn what this means: I desire mercy and not sacrifice. For I didn't come to call the righteous, but sinners."*

Matthew's purpose in his Gospel was to show how Jesus fulfilled God's promises found in the Old Testament by offering a new way of life. Here we see where Jesus healed a man and engaged in an ongoing confrontation with the Pharisees, who refused to recognize His authority and power.

Blinded by their own sense of piety and arrogance, the Pharisees thought they were the only ones in right standing with God. Hence, they were openly critical of Jesus for eating and interacting with people who did not keep the ritual sacrifices as they did. Jesus responded by calling their attention to the words of the prophet Hosea (6:6). God is more interested in a person's loyal love than He is the ritual of sacrifice. Sacrifices are worthless when given to the Lord without mercy toward others.

Christians live in a world that does not always appreciate our sense of what is right, our faith convictions, and our commitment to a godly lifestyle. We must be strong in our faith and live the life we know God wants us to live. At the same time, we must guard against developing an attitude similar to that of the Pharisees where we act like we are better than those who do not believe, act, or think as we do.

Jesus came to save humble sinners, not the self-righteous who fail so see their need for Him. For this we can be eternally grateful. Like Jesus, we are to reach out to sinners so that they may know Jesus' grace, love, and mercy.

Mark 6:1–6
I Knew You When

He went away from there and came to His home-
town, and His disciples followed Him. When the
Sabbath came, He began to teach in the syna-
gogue, and many who heard Him were astonished.
"Where did this man get these things?" they said.
"What is this wisdom given to Him, and how are
these miracles performed by His hands? Isn't this
the carpenter, the son of Mary, and the brother
of James, Joses, Judas, and Simon? And aren't His
sisters here with us?" So they were offended by Him.

Then Jesus said to them, "A prophet is not
without honor except in his hometown, among his
relatives, and in his household." So He was not able
to do any miracles there, except that He laid His
hands on a few sick people and healed them. And
He was amazed at their unbelief.

A pastor's son attended seminary, and his dad's church asked the son to preach one weekend when his father was out of town. Those who were new to the church thought he preached well and were moved by His sermon and what God stirred in their hearts through the teaching of the Word. But those who had seen the little boy grow up in the church had trouble seeing this young man as a preacher. To them, he was still the little kid who purposefully picked his nose during the preschool Christmas program, mooned the ladies' prayer group when he was ten, and later got caught throwing a party with alcohol when his parents were away. They had a hard time seeing him as something other than a rambunctious child who liked to stretch (or break) the rules.

A similar thing happened to Jesus in the passage on the previous page. The people of Nazareth knew Him well, they thought. Sure, they had heard that His birth was unique, but they assumed the stories were just that—stories. They had watched Him run in the streets as a boy. They watched Him grow into a young man, gaining the skills of a carpenter and working hard at His craft.

But now, they had heard He was teaching spiritual truth like none before Him. They had even heard He was healing the sick and casting out demons. Rather than come to Him, they took offense at Him. How could one of their own be telling them how to follow God? They missed His truth and His miracles because they believed He was no different than they were.

Maybe you know somebody who believes that Jesus was not the Son of God. Perhaps you have friends who don't accept that Jesus actually worked miracles. "He was just a man like us," some think. But we know He wasn't, and we know they need Him. Take time now to pray that those who do not believe Jesus is the Son of God will learn the truth and decide to follow Him.

Mark 6:7–12
God Will Provide

He summoned the Twelve and began to send them out in pairs and gave them authority over unclean spirits. He instructed them to take nothing for the road except a walking stick: no bread, no traveling bag, no money in their belts. They were to wear sandals, but not put on an extra shirt. Then He said to them, "Whenever you enter a house, stay there until you leave that place. If any place does not welcome you and people refuse to listen to you, when you leave there, shake the dust off your feet as a testimony against them."

So they went out and preached that people should repent.

A young couple prayerfully considers God's call to international missions. They accept the call and begin to make preparations with a brand-new sending agency. But they're shocked when they learn about some of the agency's policies. First, the couple discovers they are not allowed to take any of their belongings with them—including extra clothes. This seems odd, but they figure it must be cheaper to buy new things in their new country than to pay to ship their own things. They come to terms with this idea. But then they discover that the sending agency won't be providing any financial support, and the couple isn't allowed to raise any support on their own. They can take no money with them; they have to simply trust God to provide when they get there. Wait, what?

That sounds ludicrous, doesn't it? But Jesus asked His disciples to do something similar, though on a smaller scale. It was an exercise in faith for the disciples. They were to take no bag, no bread, nor money on this mission, but to rely on the Lord to provide everything for them. With no means to buy food and no bread to nourish them, they would learn that when they hungered, the Lord Himself would provide. When they needed clean clothing, God would provide. When they needed anything, God would provide.

The thought of trusting in God to completely provide like this sounds both logical and crazy. Why wouldn't He provide, right? He's God. But don't we hold some responsibility for ourselves? Are we really just supposed to rely on others to support us? That's not really the point here, though. It's about trusting in His provision, however He chooses to do that.

There is freedom in not relying upon our possessions or our wealth. It opens our eyes to where everything comes from and fosters generosity. Gratitude for God's provision deepens, and drives us to tend to others' needs, not just our own. As we travel this world, let us hold loosely that which can be taken away in a moment, and hold tightly to the One who keeps His promises. Let's travel lightly so that our hands are available to help others and show His love all the more!

Matthew 11:25–30
His Yoke Is Easy

At that time Jesus said, "I praise You, Father, Lord of heaven and earth, because You have hidden these things from the wise and learned and revealed them to infants. Yes, Father, because this was Your good pleasure. All things have been entrusted to Me by My Father. No one knows the Son except the Father, and no one knows the Father except the Son and anyone to whom the Son desires to reveal Him.

"Come to Me, all of you who are weary and burdened, and I will give you rest. All of you, take up My yoke and learn from Me, because I am gentle and humble in heart, and you will find rest for yourselves. For My yoke is easy and My burden is light."

In Laura Ingalls Wilder's book *Farmer Boy*, there is a scene where young Almanzo receives a yoke for his two calves, Star and Bright. He struggles to teach the young animals how to work together in the apparatus. They're not used to it, and they continue to get tangled and twisted up. But as he patiently works with them, they start to get the hang of it. They will learn, and they will someday be able to pull a plow or a wagon. But the most important thing about Almanzo's yoke might be in its description. His father created it out of red cedar, which meant it was strong, but it was also lightweight. The young calves would easily be able to use it. It will not be a burden to them.

In New Testament times, the yoke was a common metaphor for one person's subjection to another. In Judaism, a yoke also referred to the law. It was burdensome, because the Old Testament contained a host of laws, and the Pharisees had created thousands more, and it was impossible to keep them all. In fact, it was likely impossible to keep very many of them. It was an act of futility.

Jesus knows the laboring of the human heart. He is intimately acquainted with our struggles, doubts, fears, and guilt. And He sees the pull that legalism's yoke holds on our hearts. So He offers relief in the form of another yoke—His own.

The yoke of rules is heavy; the yoke of Jesus is light. The yoke of legalism oppresses us; the yoke of Jesus relieves us. The yoke of the law says, "Work for me." The yoke of Jesus says, "Rest in Me."

We rest in Jesus by surrendering our hearts to Him. After surrendering to Jesus, we learn from Jesus, and He is patient with us, just as Almanzo was patient with his calves. We learn from Jesus by meditating on His Word. When meditating on His Word, we respond by praying. This is God's way of rejuvenating the soul. Know and learn the way of rest.

Luke 6:1-11
Lord of the Sabbath

On a Sabbath, He passed through the grainfields. His disciples were picking heads of grain, rubbing them in their hands, and eating them. But some of the Pharisees said, "Why are you doing what is not lawful on the Sabbath?"

Jesus answered them, "Haven't you read what David and those who were with him did when he was hungry—how he entered the house of God, and took and ate the sacred bread, which is not lawful for any but the priests to eat? He even gave some to those who were with him." Then He told them, "The Son of Man is Lord of the Sabbath."

On another Sabbath He entered the synagogue and was teaching. A man was there whose right hand was paralyzed. The scribes and Pharisees were watching Him closely, to see if He would heal on the Sabbath, so that they could find a charge against Him. But He knew their thoughts and told the man with the paralyzed hand, "Get up and stand here." So he got up and stood there. Then Jesus said to them, "I ask you: Is it lawful on the Sabbath to do what is good or to do what is evil, to save life or to destroy it?" After looking around at them all, He told him, "Stretch out your hand." He did so, and his hand was restored. They, however, were filled with rage and started discussing with one another what they might do to Jesus.

The religious leaders had a habit of confronting Jesus concerning practices that, in their opinion, showed His disregard for the legal religious code. Their scrutiny was designed to bring an accusation against Him. Jesus knew their intentions, however, and confronted them head on.

In these verses, the Pharisees challenged Him about breaking the Sabbath. At the time, there were numerous and detailed religious laws about what people were allowed to do and not do on the Sabbath. The Pharisees were determined to charge Jesus with breaking one of these laws.

In healing the man with the deformed hand, Jesus was moved by a desire to do good. The religious leaders were driven by a desire to destroy. Thus, Jesus challenged their thinking with the question posed in verse 9. How could they possibly think a plot to bring Jesus harm was more appropriate than His purpose to make a man whole? How could they justify elevating religious tradition over doing what was best for a person in need?

Christians, individually and collectively as a church, need to be on guard that our commitment to religious practices and traditions do not overshadow our calling to be like Jesus. He acted in the best interest of every individual He encountered, all the way to the cross.

Luke 6:20–23, 27–36
Say What?

Then looking up at His disciples, He said:

You who are poor are blessed, because the kingdom of God is yours. You who are now hungry are blessed, because you will be filled. You who now weep are blessed, because you will laugh. You are blessed when people hate you, when they exclude you, insult you, and slander your name as evil because of the Son of Man.

"Rejoice in that day and leap for joy! Take note—your reward is great in heaven, for this is the way their ancestors used to treat the prophets. . . .

"But I say to you who listen: Love your enemies, do what is good to those who hate you, bless those who curse you, pray for those who mistreat you. If anyone hits you on the cheek, offer the other also. And if anyone takes away your coat, don't hold back your shirt either. Give to everyone who asks you, and from one who takes your things, don't ask for them back. Just as you want others to do for you, do the same for them. If you love those who love you, what credit is that to you? Even sinners love those who love them. If you do what is good to those who are good to you, what credit is that to you? Even sinners do that. And if you lend to those from whom you expect to receive, what credit is that to you? Even sinners lend to sinners to

> *be repaid in full. But love your enemies, do what is*
> *good, and lend, expecting nothing in return. Then*
> *your reward will be great, and you will be sons of*
> *the Most High. For He is gracious to the ungrate-*
> *ful and evil. Be merciful, just as your Father also is*
> *merciful."*

These verses seem to be full of contradictions and flat-out illogical commands. What Jesus proposed appears illogical. When others hate me, I should be happy? When I'm left out, I should be glad? I should love my enemies? When somebody hits me, I should just tempt them to do it again? I should give more than people ask for?

Yet the key phrase in these verses is "because of the Son of Man." When we so identify with Jesus that others hate us, ostracize us, and speak evil of us, Jesus says we are blessed. In fact, we are in good company with the prophets of old. And when we act and react in a positive manner that's contrary to what people expect, we show them who the Son of Man truly is.

Only with a proper view of circumstances can a negative experience give birth to a blessing. When we identify with Christ, opposition will arise from various and sometimes surprising sources. Joy is possible, however, when we remember that we are suffering for a good cause—the name of Christ.

Matthew 12:33–37
Words Matter

*Either make the tree good and its fruit good,
or make the tree bad and its fruit bad; for a tree
is known by its fruit. Brood of vipers! How can
you speak good things when you are evil? For the
mouth speaks from the overflow of the heart. A
good man produces good things from his storeroom of good, and an evil man produces evil
things from his storeroom of evil. I tell you that on
the day of judgment people will have to account
for every careless word they speak. For by your
words you will be acquitted, and by your words
you will be condemned.*

What is in a word? How about power?

Jesus said that your words have the power to acquit or condemn you. He said this to Pharisees who suggested that He drove out
demons by Beelzebul, the ruler of the demons. They were saying, in
effect, that the Spirit in Jesus was a demon. This reflected the reality of
their hearts, indicating that they did not know the Lord; so their words
actually condemned them.

The Pharisees were constantly criticizing Jesus in public, tearing
Him down, and causing people to doubt the truth that came from
Jesus' lips. Jesus said it is impossible for good fruit to come from an
evil tree.

Words have the power to injure or to build. We know the child's proverb: "Sticks and stones may break my bones, but words will never hurt me." We also know that is not true. Words can injure and maim the human spirit. Consider these words, for example: idiot, stupid, imbecile, loser. Imagine them being said about you or to you. In fact, you may not have to imagine, because it happens to you on a regular basis. Then, consider these words: friend, thoughtful, wise, happy, faithful. If these are said to you or about you, how would that make you feel? Words have the power to injure or to build up.

In this electronic age, words fly around the world in a flash. People e-mail, text, and tweet with abandon, reacting and overreacting to everything from what's taking place in their own backyard to events on the other side of the world. Some people post Scripture or inspirational thoughts on social media. Others post hateful words to friends who hold different political views than they do, to the schoolmate they are bullying, or to complete strangers. Hardly a day passes without some famous person trying to take back harsh words they spoke carelessly.

Words matter. Like stones, they can build up or tear down. Jesus said that we are the tree and our words are our fruit. The words we speak—or write or text—reveal who we really are on the inside.

Words match the heart—good or evil. And by those words we will be judged. Let's leave the careless words unsaid and strive for acquittal, not condemnation.

Mark 6:30-44
So Much More

The apostles gathered around Jesus and reported to Him all that they had done and taught. He said to them, "Come away by yourselves to a remote place and rest for a while." For many people were coming and going, and they did not even have time to eat. So they went away in the boat by themselves to a remote place, but many saw them leaving and recognized them. People ran there by land from all the towns and arrived ahead of them. So as He stepped ashore, He saw a huge crowd and had compassion on them, because they were like sheep without a shepherd. Then He began to teach them many things.

When it was already late, His disciples approached Him and said, "This place is a wilderness, and it is already late! Send them away, so they can go into the surrounding countryside and villages to buy themselves something to eat."

"You give them something to eat," He responded.

They said to Him, "Should we go and buy 200 denarii worth of bread and give them something to eat?"

And He asked them, "How many loaves do you have? Go look."

When they found out they said, "Five, and two fish."

Then He instructed them to have all the people sit down in groups on the green grass. So they sat down in ranks of hundreds and fifties. Then He took the five loaves and the two fish, and looking up to heaven, He blessed and broke the loaves. He kept giving them to His disciples to set before the people. He also divided the two fish among them all. Everyone ate and was filled. Then they picked up 12 baskets full of pieces of bread and fish. Now those who ate the loaves were 5,000 men.

The miracle of the feeding of the 5,000 (though the number would have been much higher if you count women and children) is the only miracle that is recorded in all four Gospel accounts, aside from Jesus' resurrection. Since the Holy Spirit deemed it important enough to inspire all four writers to include it, we have to infer that it contains some pretty big truths.

This story blatantly shows Jesus' power. The people had seen over and over again how He could heal people from diseases. But to miraculously multiply food? Jesus was blatantly showing His disciples—and anyone else who cared to notice—that He was truly the Messiah.

Jesus showed the importance of not only caring for people's spiritual needs, but also their physical ones. He didn't always do both, but a careful examination of the Gospels will reveal that He often did, and this case is no exception. We would do well to imitate Him in this.

This event also reveals that even when we give Jesus a little, He can turn it into a lot. We rarely think on such a grand scale as this story. We might expect some increase to what we give, but Jesus is capable and willing to turn it into so much more!

Mark 7:1–13
Following God or Tradition?

The Pharisees and some of the scribes who had come from Jerusalem gathered around Him. They observed that some of His disciples were eating their bread with unclean—that is, unwashed—hands. (For the Pharisees, in fact all the Jews, will not eat unless they wash their hands ritually, keeping the tradition of the elders. When they come from the marketplace, they do not eat unless they have washed. And there are many other customs they have received and keep, like the washing of cups, jugs, copper utensils, and dining couches.) Then the Pharisees and the scribes asked Him, "Why don't Your disciples live according to the tradition of the elders, instead of eating bread with ritually unclean hands?"

He answered them, "Isaiah prophesied correctly about you hypocrites, as it is written:

These people honor Me with their lips, but their heart is far from Me. They worship Me in vain, teaching as doctrines the commands of men.

Disregarding the command of God, you keep the tradition of men." He also said to them, "You completely invalidate God's command in order to maintain your tradition! For Moses said:

Honor your father and your mother; and

Whoever speaks evil of father or mother must be put to death.

> *But you say, 'If a man tells his father or mother:*
> *Whatever benefit you might have received from me*
> *is Corban'" (that is, a gift committed to the temple),*
> *"you no longer let him do anything for his father*
> *or mother. You revoke God's word by your tradition*
> *that you have handed down. And you do many*
> *other similar things."*

Jesus had quite a bit to say to the Pharisees here. Most of us are well aware of the fact that the Pharisees added many laws to the ones laid out in Scripture, and they also extended existing laws farther than they were intended to go. For example, Scripture only declared that a priest had to wash his hands at the moment of sacrifice at the temple, but the Pharisees had extended that law to say that all Jews had to wash their hands before eating anything.

What is not often talked about, however, is what Jesus points out in the Scriptures above. The Pharisees had also gone so far into making and keeping their traditional laws that they sometimes nullified God's true laws. As Jesus described above, God had made two pretty strong commands about honoring our parents. But the Pharisees had put a law in place that would allow people to circumvent those laws. Let's paraphrase the statement above about Corban into something we can understand: "If you tell your parents you can't support them because your money is reserved for God [Corban], then you revoke God's Word for a tradition."

Do we do this? Do we add to God's Word? Do we create traditional "laws" for Christians that actually nullify God's true commands to us? Likely we all have done this, in one way or another. Take some time right now to consider whether you are following God or tradition.

Matthew 13:24–30, 36–43
Weeds

*He presented another parable to them: "The king-
dom of heaven may be compared to a man who
sowed good seed in his field. But while people
were sleeping, his enemy came, sowed weeds
among the wheat, and left. When the plants
sprouted and produced grain, then the weeds also
appeared. The landowner's slaves came to him and
said, 'Master, didn't you sow good seed in your
field? Then where did the weeds come from?'*

"'An enemy did this!' he told them.

*"'So, do you want us to go and gather them
up?' the slaves asked him.*

*"'No,' he said. 'When you gather up the weeds,
you might also uproot the wheat with them. Let
both grow together until the harvest. At harvest
time I'll tell the reapers: Gather the weeds first and
tie them in bundles to burn them, but store the
wheat in my barn.'" . . .*

*Then He dismissed the crowds and went into
the house. His disciples approached Him and
said, "Explain the parable of the weeds in the field
to us."*

*He replied: "The One who sows the good seed
is the Son of Man; the field is the world; and the
good seed—these are the sons of the kingdom.
The weeds are the sons of the evil one, and the*

enemy who sowed them is the Devil. The harvest is
the end of the age, and the harvesters are angels.
Therefore, just as the weeds are gathered and
burned in the fire, so it will be at the end of the
age. The Son of Man will send out His angels, and
they will gather from His kingdom everything that
causes sin and those guilty of lawlessness. They will
throw them into the blazing furnace where there
will be weeping and gnashing of teeth. Then the
righteous will shine like the sun in their Father's king-
dom. Anyone who has ears should listen!

If you grew up on a farm or with a garden, you learned to despise weeds. Hours in the broiling sun with a hoe in your hands help you sympathize with farmers who will do anything to get rid of the things.

Over the years the attempts to kill them have included some strong pesticides that killed not only the weeds but also good crops. Some of the pesticides even endangered our health.

In truth, some weeds are quite useful, producing nectar for the bees, improving the soil's nutrients, even providing ingredients for salads. In the divine plan of the Father, everything has its purpose.

Other "weeds" will show their true colors at the harvest. Jesus made that point in His parable. Our job isn't to identify those we may consider the "weeds" and judge them as such. Only He will judge who is gathered to heaven and who is tossed into the fire.

Luke 7:36–50
Our Debt Is Paid

Then one of the Pharisees invited Him to eat with him. He entered the Pharisee's house and reclined at the table. And a woman in the town who was a sinner found out that Jesus was reclining at the table in the Pharisee's house. She brought an alabaster jar of fragrant oil and stood behind Him at His feet, weeping, and began to wash His feet with her tears. She wiped His feet with the hair of her head, kissing them and anointing them with the fragrant oil.

When the Pharisee who had invited Him saw this, he said to himself, "This man, if He were a prophet, would know who and what kind of woman this is who is touching Him—she's a sinner!"

Jesus replied to him, "Simon, I have something to say to you."

"Teacher," he said, "say it."

"A creditor had two debtors. One owed 500 denarii, and the other 50. Since they could not pay it back, he graciously forgave them both. So, which of them will love him more?"

Simon answered, "I suppose the one he forgave more."

"You have judged correctly," He told him. Turning to the woman, He said to Simon, "Do you see this woman? I entered your house; you gave Me no water for My feet, but she, with her tears,

has washed My feet and wiped them with her hair. You gave Me no kiss, but she hasn't stopped kissing My feet since I came in. You didn't anoint My head with olive oil, but she has anointed My feet with fragrant oil. Therefore I tell you, her many sins have been forgiven; that's why she loved much. But the one who is forgiven little, loves little." Then He said to her, "Your sins are forgiven."

Those who were at the table with Him began to say among themselves, "Who is this man who even forgives sins?"

And He said to the woman, "Your faith has saved you. Go in peace."

Once we grasp the depth of pain or sorrow we caused someone, we agonize about how to make it right. When we understand the enormity of that debt, we begin to grasp the priceless gift of forgiveness.

The woman in today's passage understood the depth of her sin. She could never undo wrongful choices or harmful deeds; she needed cleansing from the inside out. Jesus welcomed her and His forgiveness overwhelmed her, and He changed her life. He loved much and forgave.

Jesus set the standard for forgiveness by paying a price the offender, the sinner, could never afford. Jesus faced death for our transgressions: "He was pierced because of our transgressions, crushed because of our iniquities . . . and we are healed by His wounds" (Isa. 53:5).

Consider the debt Jesus paid for you. Remember how it feels to be forgiven. Recall things known only to you and God, and humbly love Him in gratitude for what He has done. Now, our challenge is to forgive others as He has forgiven us. If we love much, we will also forgive much.

John 10:7–18
The Good Shepherd

So Jesus said again, "I assure you: I am the door of the sheep. All who came before Me are thieves and robbers, but the sheep didn't listen to them. I am the door. If anyone enters by Me, he will be saved and will come in and go out and find pasture. A thief comes only to steal and to kill and to destroy. I have come so that they may have life and have it in abundance.

"I am the good shepherd. The good shepherd lays down his life for the sheep. The hired man, since he is not the shepherd and doesn't own the sheep, leaves them and runs away when he sees a wolf coming. The wolf then snatches and scatters them. This happens because he is a hired man and doesn't care about the sheep.

"I am the good shepherd. I know My own sheep, and they know Me, as the Father knows Me, and I know the Father. I lay down My life for the sheep. But I have other sheep that are not of this fold; I must bring them also, and they will listen to My voice. Then there will be one flock, one shepherd. This is why the Father loves Me, because I am laying down My life so I may take it up again. No one takes it from Me, but I lay it down on My own. I have the right to lay it down, and I have the right

*to take it up again. I have received this command
from My Father."*

Most people do not understand the role of a Palestinian shepherd. This job typically required long hours and lots of work. The sheep were normally exposed to the danger of wild animals and thieves. This means that a shepherd had to maintain a consistent, patient love for his sheep.

One of the greatest images of Jesus is found in this passage as Jesus shows that He is the Good Shepherd, fulfilling Ezekiel 34:23. The same audience that's in chapter 9 is also in chapter 10; therefore, Jesus is saying this in the presence of the religious leaders of His time. Just like Ezekiel 34, the religious leaders were less like shepherds protecting their flock and more like predators preying on their flock.

Jesus shows us the richness of Himself as the Good Shepherd. He shows us that His ultimate desire is to lay down His life for the sheep. The great part about this passage is that this promise of salvation for His sheep extends beyond Israel and to all people of any nation who receive Jesus as the Good Shepherd.

Luke 8:26–39
Go and Tell

*Then they sailed to the region of the Gerasenes,
which is opposite Galilee. When He got out on
land, a demon-possessed man from the town met
Him. For a long time he had worn no clothes and
did not stay in a house but in the tombs. When
he saw Jesus, he cried out, fell down before Him,
and said in a loud voice, "What do You have to
do with me, Jesus, You Son of the Most High God?
I beg You, don't torment me!" For He had commanded the unclean spirit to come out of the man.
Many times it had seized him, and though he was
guarded, bound by chains and shackles, he would
snap the restraints and be driven by the demon
into deserted places.*

"What is your name?" Jesus asked him.

*"Legion," he said—because many demons had
entered him. And they begged Him not to banish
them to the abyss.*

*A large herd of pigs was there, feeding on the
hillside. The demons begged Him to permit them
to enter the pigs, and He gave them permission.
The demons came out of the man and entered the
pigs, and the herd rushed down the steep bank
into the lake and drowned. When the men who
tended them saw what had happened, they ran off
and reported it in the town and in the countryside.*

> *Then people went out to see what had hap-*
> *pened. They came to Jesus and found the man the*
> *demons had departed from, sitting at Jesus' feet,*
> *dressed and in his right mind. And they were afraid.*
> *Meanwhile, the eyewitnesses reported to them how*
> *the demon-possessed man was delivered. Then all*
> *the people of the Gerasene region asked Him to*
> *leave them, because they were gripped by great*
> *fear. So getting into the boat, He returned.*
>
> *The man from whom the demons had*
> *departed kept begging Him to be with Him. But He*
> *sent him away and said, "Go back to your home,*
> *and tell all that God has done for you." And off*
> *he went, proclaiming throughout the town all that*
> *Jesus had done for him.*

When it comes to telling nonbelievers about Jesus, a personal testimony of salvation can carry a lot of weight. People can argue with you about theology or biblical interpretation, but they can't argue with your personal experience.

In the passage above, Jesus commanded a formerly demon-possessed man to go home and tell what great things God had done for him. His friends and family knew him when he was possessed by demons. Now they would see the change in him and be amazed by his story and give God the glory.

We who have been given eternal life, who have experienced His transforming power, and who are indwelt by His Spirit, have a story to tell. When the substance of our lives matches the stories of our lips, God will use our testimonies to draw others to Himself.

Matthew 14:22–33
Confidence in Christ

Immediately He made the disciples get into the boat and go ahead of Him to the other side, while He dismissed the crowds. After dismissing the crowds, He went up on the mountain by Himself to pray. When evening came, He was there alone. But the boat was already over a mile from land, battered by the waves, because the wind was against them. Around three in the morning, He came toward them walking on the sea. When the disciples saw Him walking on the sea, they were terrified. "It's a ghost!" they said, and cried out in fear.

Immediately Jesus spoke to them. "Have courage! It is I. Don't be afraid."

"Lord, if it's You," Peter answered Him, "command me to come to You on the water."

"Come!" He said.

And climbing out of the boat, Peter started walking on the water and came toward Jesus. But when he saw the strength of the wind, he was afraid. And beginning to sink he cried out, "Lord, save me!"

Immediately Jesus reached out His hand, caught hold of him, and said to him, "You of little faith, why did you doubt?" When they got into the boat, the wind ceased. Then those in the boat worshiped Him and said, "Truly You are the Son of God!"

Jesus came to bring us peace. In fact, He is called the Prince of Peace. The wrath and judgment of God against sin may promote fear in the heart to draw us to Him. But the end result is that we can have peace with God and confidence of spending eternity with Him.

Many people go through life living in fear. Some people are deathly afraid of spiders. Others fear commitment. Many fear falling or flying, and some fear the future. But with Jesus, we do not have to live with the fear of death and judgment.

The disciples saw what they thought was an apparition coming toward them in the night, walking on top of the water. Who can blame them for their fear? Yet it was Jesus, and He spoke to them to calm their fear.

Moments later, Peter stepped out of the boat in faith, but he quickly became scared when he realized how strong the wind was. But he called out to Jesus, who immediately came to his rescue. What's important to note, though, is that Jesus didn't accuse Peter of having no faith at all. He said he had "little faith." But even when we have little faith, Jesus reaches out to us when we call to Him.

However, the overall message is clear: When Jesus is with us, we can be confident in any situation; we have no reason to be afraid. He will see us through any predicament or malady because we have His promise that He will never leave us. Our future is secure in Christ, and even death has no power over us. He is the Prince of Peace.

Mark 8:27–30

I Need an Answer

Jesus went out with His disciples to the villages of Caesarea Philippi. And on the road He asked His disciples, "Who do people say that I am?"

They answered Him, "John the Baptist; others, Elijah; still others, one of the prophets."

"But you," He asked them again, "who do you say that I am?"

Peter answered Him, "You are the Messiah!"

And He strictly warned them to tell no one about Him.

Nearly every American has watched the *The Price Is Right.* One of the most commonly uttered phrases on the show is likely, "I need an answer." What precedes that command? Hundreds of audience members shouting out various options to the contestant, and most of the time it's doubtful any of them are sure of the correct answer themselves. But they're sure excited to tell the contestant—and the millions of people watching—what they think the answer is. After listening to the cacophony for five or ten seconds, the host demands a response. The contestant really wants to get it right, because a correct answer could result in a new car or a washing machine or a grandfather clock.

How does the contestant know who to listen to? There are so many voices clamoring for her attention. She has to pick an answer, and everyone wants her to get it right.

When Jesus asked His disciples who they thought He was, He wanted them to get it right. He wanted them to know Who He is, why He came, and what that meant for the near and distant future. Their destiny and that of generations to come hinged on the correct answer.

Like the aforementioned contestant, the disciples had heard a lot of answers to Jesus' question. There were many voices giving their opinions on who they thought Jesus was: John the Baptist, Elijah, one of the prophets. On the other side of the coin, there were voices saying He was a sham, a tool of the Devil, a blasphemer. How was one to know which answer was correct?

When it comes down to it, a game-show contestant can try to listen for a few audience voices she trusts, but she ultimately must make the decision herself based on past experience with the product at hand. Peter's answer wasn't reliant upon the many outside voices of the day. It was based on His experiences with the man asking the question. "You are the Messiah!" he said. Cue the game show music and confetti!

Each of us must answer Jesus' question. Who do we say He is? Getting it right may not result in wealth or fame. Indeed, we may suffer persecution and rejection instead. The prize, however, makes fistfuls of money seem like small change: God's unfailing love and protection, Jesus' once-for-all redemption by way of the cross, and the day-to-day guidance offered by the Holy Spirit.

Luke 9:21-27
Take Up Your Cross

But He strictly warned and instructed them to tell this to no one, saying, "The Son of Man must suffer many things and be rejected by the elders, chief priests, and scribes, be killed, and be raised the third day."

Then He said to them all, "If anyone wants to come with Me, he must deny himself, take up his cross daily, and follow Me. For whoever wants to save his life will lose it, but whoever loses his life because of Me will save it. What is a man benefited if he gains the whole world, yet loses or forfeits himself? For whoever is ashamed of Me and My words, the Son of Man will be ashamed of him when He comes in His glory and that of the Father and the holy angels. I tell you the truth: There are some standing here who will not taste death until they see the kingdom of God."

Knowing some details of what Jesus went through at His crucifixion, we may shudder to think He might ever call us to do the same. The cross reminds us of suffering, pain, rejection, scorn, self-sacrifice, hardship, and even loving and forgiving those who have harmed us. Yet in Luke 9:23, Jesus is calling us to do just that. Jesus wants us, as His followers, to lay aside our own gain for the sake of others and for His glory. And we have His power and grace to carry us through.

Nineteenth-century pastor Charles Spurgeon said,

Mark then, Christian, Jesus does not suffer so as to exclude your suffering. He bears a cross, not that you may escape it, but that you may endure it. Christ exempts you from sin, but not from sorrow. Remember that, and expect to suffer. But let us comfort ourselves with this thought, that in our case, . . . it is not our cross, but Christ's cross which we carry. When you are molested for your piety; when your religion brings the trial of cruel mockings upon you, then remember it is not your cross, it is Christ's cross; and how delightful is it to carry the cross of our Lord Jesus! You carry the cross after him. You have blessed company; your path is marked with the footprints of your Lord. The mark of his blood-red shoulder is upon that heavy burden. 'Tis his cross, and he goes before you as a shepherd goes before his sheep. Take up your cross daily, and follow him.

Our inclination is to use our skills, talents, and resources to further our cause and gratify our own pleasures. Yet, Jesus is calling us to do something we consider radical. He calls us to identify with Him and obey His commands, regardless of the cost.

The world teaches us to do just the opposite. Today's media push us to give our preferences priority. But to follow Jesus, we must do what He did—to serve and not seek to be served. Then we will truly be His disciples.

Quote: Charles Spurgeon, *Morning and Evening*, April 5.

Luke 9:57–62
Look Forward

As they were traveling on the road someone said to Him, "I will follow You wherever You go!"

Jesus told him, "Foxes have dens, and birds of the sky have nests, but the Son of Man has no place to lay His head." Then He said to another, "Follow Me."

"Lord," he said, "first let me go bury my father."

But He told him, "Let the dead bury their own dead, but you go and spread the news of the kingdom of God."

Another also said, "I will follow You, Lord, but first let me go and say good-bye to those at my house."

But Jesus said to him, "No one who puts his hand to the plow and looks back is fit for the kingdom of God."

Some have used the passage above to justify neglecting family duties for the sake of Christ. This is wrongheaded. Jesus wasn't saying family is not important; He was saying that when we follow Him, our supreme loyalties must shift. But the men didn't understand this; they were more interested in making excuses for not following Him.

The first man in the passage was told that if he were to follow Jesus, it would be difficult. Jesus challenged the second man to make

God's kingdom his first priority. The third man was told that looking back was not a viable option.

In the days of an agrarian society, many readers of this passage would have understood what Jesus meant by putting your hand to the plow and looking back. But today's readers are mostly in the dark. Whether standing behind a plow or sitting in a tractor in front of a plow, it is impossible for a farmer to plow a straight furrow without fixing his eyes on a specific spot in front of him and aiming for it. If he looks back, he will go off course. (Note to technologically savvy farmers: Forget about GPS-guided tractors for the sake of this point!)

In the same way, there can be no looking back in our service to Jesus. There is no place for procrastination, indecision, or excuses. The job at hand demands our full concentration and dedicated service, or we will waver off course.

However, that's much easier said than done. How often have we taken our eyes off of following Jesus and made excuses for our less-than-stellar attempts? Perhaps that's why Jesus wants us to keep looking forward instead of backward. Only when our focus is on the Author and Finisher of our faith can we become all He wants us to be.

Mark 10:23–31
The Last Don't Lose

Jesus looked around and said to His disciples, "How hard it is for those who have wealth to enter the kingdom of God!" But the disciples were astonished at His words. Again Jesus said to them, "Children, how hard it is to enter the kingdom of God! It is easier for a camel to go through the eye of a needle than for a rich person to enter the kingdom of God."

So they were even more astonished, saying to one another, "Then who can be saved?"

Looking at them, Jesus said, "With men it is impossible, but not with God, because all things are possible with God."

Peter began to tell Him, "Look, we have left everything and followed You."

"I assure you," Jesus said, "there is no one who has left house, brothers or sisters, mother or father, children, or fields because of Me and the gospel, who will not receive 100 times more, now at this time—houses, brothers and sisters, mothers and children, and fields, with persecutions—and eternal life in the age to come. But many who are first will be last, and the last first."

Ours is a culture of celebrity and excess. Movie stars, singers, professional athletes, and authors all garner our applause. The rich and famous hold much influence in our society. To us, fame and money equates importance.

But Jesus turns our culture's ethic upside down with a paradox. It is not fame or money that translates importance in God's kingdom. In fact, those things can easily distract us and make it difficult for us to see our need for the Savior.

More often than not, greatness in the kingdom of God is seen in the obscure. We see it in Scripture when the shepherds were the first to hear about Jesus' birth. We see it when Jesus called fishermen to be His disciples. We see it when a woman was the first person to see Jesus alive after His resurrection.

In today's world, it's the widow who sacrificially gives to the missions offering. It's the young mother who mentors a teenager or the veteran pastor who serves his people. It's the missionary who serves an African village and in a wealthy CEO who lavishly gives to make the gospel known. It's the person with a disability who volunteers in the church nursery.

You see, greatness in the kingdom is not about how rich you are or how polished you are on the outside; it's about how broken you are on the inside. It's ultimately a matter of the heart. That might mean you're viewed as last in the eyes of the world. But on God's playing field, the last don't lose.

Luke 10:25–37
Love Your Neighbor

Just then an expert in the law stood up to test Him, saying, "Teacher, what must I do to inherit eternal life?"

"What is written in the law?" He asked him. "How do you read it?"

He answered:

Love the Lord your God with all your heart, with all your soul, with all your strength, and with all your mind; and your neighbor as yourself.

"You've answered correctly," He told him. "Do this and you will live."

But wanting to justify himself, he asked Jesus, "And who is my neighbor?"

Jesus took up the question and said: "A man was going down from Jerusalem to Jericho and fell into the hands of robbers. They stripped him, beat him up, and fled, leaving him half dead. A priest happened to be going down that road. When he saw him, he passed by on the other side. In the same way, a Levite, when he arrived at the place and saw him, passed by on the other side. But a Samaritan on his journey came up to him, and when he saw the man, he had compassion. He went over to him and bandaged his wounds, pouring on olive oil and wine. Then he put him on his own animal, brought him to an inn, and took care of him. The next day he took out two denarii, gave them to the innkeeper, and said, 'Take care of him. When I come back I'll reimburse you for whatever extra you spend.'

"Which of these three do you think proved to be a neighbor to the man who fell into the hands of the robbers?"

"The one who showed mercy to him," he said. Then Jesus told him, "Go and do the same."

This passage starts out with a short discussion on the greatest commandments. Jesus put the lawyer on the spot, and he got the answer right: Love God with everything within you, and love your neighbor as yourself. But he wanted some clarification: Just who is my neighbor?

And, true to form, Jesus responded with a story instead of a pat answer. He knew that the man would only consider other righteous Jews to be his neighbor. But Jesus blew that theory right out of the water. In this story, the two men who would have culturally been considered a neighbor—the priest and the Levite—actually ignored the man. It was his enemy—a wicked Samaritan, of all people—who helped him.

We all have a tendency to want to help those who are like us. We're comfortable with them, we can put ourselves in their shoes, and for the most part it's easy. But it's a little more difficult when the need is borne by someone who is different, who worships a false God, who might be dirty or poor or of another race.

But like the Samaritan, we need to put aside all those ideas of who our neighbor is and reach out to anyone who is in need. Who do you see that's in need in your neighborhood? Make a decision now to see everyone as your neighbor, and then be proactive about helping anyone in need.

Mark 10:46–52
Healing Faith

They came to Jericho. And as He was leaving Jericho with His disciples and a large crowd, Bartimaeus (the son of Timaeus), a blind beggar, was sitting by the road. When he heard that it was Jesus the Nazarene, he began to cry out, "Son of David, Jesus, have mercy on me!" Many people told him to keep quiet, but he was crying out all the more, "Have mercy on me, Son of David!"

Jesus stopped and said, "Call him."

So they called the blind man and said to him, "Have courage! Get up; He's calling for you." He threw off his coat, jumped up, and came to Jesus.

Then Jesus answered him, "What do you want Me to do for you?"

"Rabbouni," the blind man told Him, "I want to see!"

"Go your way," Jesus told him. "Your faith has healed you." Immediately he could see and began to follow Him on the road.

The story of Bartimaeus shows what true faith can do. Faith is not magic. The power of faith does not come from positive thinking or emotion. It does not come from sitting by the wayside, failing to interact with God and ask Him for help. It comes from asking God to give you the good things He desires for you.

In this passage, Bartimaeus wanted two things. First, he wanted mercy. Second, he wanted to receive his sight. The Lord granted both of these things to him. As well as giving Bartimaeus his physical sight, Jesus gave him something far more important. He gave him spiritual sight, because the Bible says he began to follow Jesus. Jesus still bestows mercy and sight today.

If your faith rests in God, like Bartimaeus' faith, then your faith can accomplish amazing things, because God is all powerful. Often, we do not see the effects of our faith because we ask with selfish motives. Let's strive to be humble and unselfish and ask God to give us what is best for us and what He desires for us to have. What better prayer can we ask than that?

Do you need mercy? Do you need the ability to see God? Call on Him today. The Lord is here and ready to listen. Turn from your tendency toward self-sufficiency. Don't keep your needs hidden quietly inside yourself. Let Him hear your voice. Call out for mercy, and ask Him to heal you from your sins. He will listen, and He will act on your behalf.

Matthew 18:1–5, 10–14
The Lord's Desire

*At that time the disciples came to Jesus and said,
"Who is greatest in the kingdom of heaven?"*

*Then He called a child to Him and had him
stand among them. "I assure you," He said, "unless
you are converted and become like children, you
will never enter the kingdom of heaven. Therefore,
whoever humbles himself like this child—this one
is the greatest in the kingdom of heaven. And
whoever welcomes one child like this in My name
welcomes Me. . . .*

*"See that you don't look down on one of these
little ones, because I tell you that in heaven their
angels continually view the face of My Father in
heaven. [For the Son of Man has come to save the
lost.] What do you think? If a man has 100 sheep,
and one of them goes astray, won't he leave the
99 on the hillside and go and search for the stray?
And if he finds it, I assure you: He rejoices over that
sheep more than over the 99 that did not go astray.
In the same way, it is not the will of your Father in
heaven that one of these little ones perish."*

Jesus always welcomed women, children, lepers, and those who were
hurting. He showed great love and acceptance toward the vulnerable. In today's Christian culture, that might not sound so surprising,

but in Jesus' day, it was a radical way of thinking and living. Children, women, and the sick were to be pitied, not helped, and definitely not seen as being "greater" than the religious men of the day.

It's important to note that Jesus isn't talking to the Pharisees here, but to His disciples. It's also interesting that in the following chapter, those same disciples tried to keep children from coming to Jesus, who responded, "Leave the children alone, and don't try to keep them from coming to Me, because the kingdom of heaven is made up of people like this" (Matt. 19:14).

Going back to chapter 18, Jesus tells His followers about His Father. As a Shepherd, God goes after a lost sheep, because it is not His will that even one should perish.

What a challenge and a warning to all of us. Are we that welcoming to those who are vulnerable and hurting? Or are we easily irritated and annoyed by those who are wounded and needy? Being surrounded by children is a chaotic, fussy, clamoring business. But that is exactly where Jesus willingly placed Himself: in the mess, noise, and chaos.

He was driven by an awareness of His Father's will, so He loved the loud children and the "unclean" lepers, because He was focused on their souls. He loves people, even the most demanding, because He sees past the immediate moment into eternity. And we can follow Him and love the needy people in our lives by keeping our Father's desire in mind.

Matthew 18:15-20
The Task of Reconciliation

If your brother sins against you, go and rebuke him in private. If he listens to you, you have won your brother. But if he won't listen, take one or two more with you, so that by the testimony of two or three witnesses every fact may be established. If he pays no attention to them, tell the church. But if he doesn't pay attention even to the church, let him be like an unbeliever and a tax collector to you. I assure you: Whatever you bind on earth is already bound in heaven, and whatever you loose on earth is already loosed in heaven. Again, I assure you: If two of you on earth agree about any matter that you pray for, it will be done for you by My Father in heaven. For where two or three are gathered together in My name, I am there among them.

As believers, we are called to the task of reconciliation. Can you recall a time in the past when a relationship you once enjoyed with another person was damaged as a result of a disagreement? Perhaps harsh words were spoken or other issues arose that caused you and the other person to be at odds with one another.

In today's passage, Jesus reminds us that when someone has wronged us, we should be willing to take the initiative in restoring the relationship even though we might be the one who has been offended. Being obedient to Jesus' command to reconcile with our brothers and sisters enables us to experience the joy of a restored relationship, and it can also help the other person spiritually.

Many churches use these verses as their guidelines for church discipline. Often, Christians are tempted to just go straight to their small group, the elders, or a pastor when they have a dispute with another church member. But these verses (and wise leaders in churches) mandate that the believer first go to the other person in private. There is no need to broadcast his sins to others if he will listen to your godly rebuke. If that doesn't work, the believer is still not to take the offense to a wide group of people, but just to one or two more. Usually, by this point, the offender will heed the rebuke, and there is no need to take it any further. If he does not, then—and only then—should it be taken in front of the wider church.

But reconciliation should first be a private, individual matter. After all, we wouldn't want our sins broadcast to the entire church or community by someone we had offended, would we? We would prefer that person come to us directly and settle the matter privately.

Jesus paid the supreme sacrifice to reconcile us to God. Therefore, we are called to the ministry of reconciliation with others.

Luke 10:38-42

Service and Communion with Christ

While they were traveling, He entered a village, and a woman named Martha welcomed Him into her home. She had a sister named Mary, who also sat at the Lord's feet and was listening to what He said. But Martha was distracted by her many tasks, and she came up and asked, "Lord, don't You care that my sister has left me to serve alone? So tell her to give me a hand."

The Lord answered her, "Martha, Martha, you are worried and upset about many things, but one thing is necessary. Mary has made the right choice, and it will not be taken away from her."

Some believers have used the above passage as an excuse to not serve the Lord (or others) with their hands but instead to only focus on spiritual matters. "Jesus said it's the right choice!" they say. But we must consider what Jesus said here in light of other Scriptures where we are exhorted to serve.

Charles Spurgeon says,

The condition of a servant well becomes every Christian. "I serve," should be the motto of all the princes of the royal family of heaven. Nor was it her fault that she had "[many tasks]." We cannot do too much. Let us do all that we possibly can; let head, and heart, and hands, be engaged in the Master's service. It was no fault of hers that she was busy preparing a feast for the Master. Happy Martha, to have an opportunity of entertaining so blessed a guest; and happy, too, to have the spirit to throw her whole soul so heartily into the engagement. Her fault was that she ["was distracted"] so that she forgot him, and only remembered the service. She allowed service to override communion, and so presented one duty stained with the blood of another.

We ought to be Martha and Mary in one: we should do much service, and have much communion at the same time. For this we need great grace. It is easier to serve than to commune. . . . The choicest fruits are the hardest to rear: the most heavenly graces are the most difficult to cultivate. . . . See to it that sitting at the Saviour's feet is not neglected, even though it be under the specious pretext of doing him service. The first thing for our soul's health, the first thing for his glory, and the first thing for our own usefulness, is to keep ourselves in perpetual communion with the Lord Jesus, and to see that the vital spirituality of our religion is maintained over and above everything else in the world.

Let us strive to live a life of both service and communion with the Lord, not neglecting one for the other.

Quote: Charles Spurgeon, *Morning and Evening*, January 24.

John 11:11–27
No More Death

He told them, "Our friend Lazarus has fallen asleep, but I'm on My way to wake him up."

Then the disciples said to Him, "Lord, if he has fallen asleep, he will get well."

Jesus, however, was speaking about his death, but they thought He was speaking about natural sleep. So Jesus then told them plainly, "Lazarus has died. I'm glad for you that I wasn't there so that you may believe. But let's go to him."

Then Thomas (called "Twin") said to his fellow disciples, "Let's go so that we may die with Him."

When Jesus arrived, He found that Lazarus had already been in the tomb four days. Bethany was near Jerusalem (about two miles away).

Many of the Jews had come to Martha and Mary to comfort them about their brother. As soon as Martha heard that Jesus was coming, she went to meet Him. But Mary remained seated in the house.

Then Martha said to Jesus, "Lord, if You had been here, my brother wouldn't have died. Yet even now I know that whatever You ask from God, God will give You."

"Your brother will rise again," Jesus told her.

Martha said, "I know that he will rise again in the resurrection at the last day."

Jesus said to her, "I am the resurrection and the life. The one who believes in Me, even if he dies, will live. Everyone who lives and believes in Me will never die—ever. Do you believe this?"

"Yes, Lord," she told Him, "I believe You are the Messiah, the Son of God, who comes into the world."

Martin Luther was a monk whose teachings led to the Reformation of 1517. The most important of his rediscoveries was the biblical truth that we are saved by accepting God's grace through faith in Christ alone, rather than by performing religious works. For this reason, he had great faith in the promise of eternal life.

Luther's teenaged daughter Magdalena was struck with illness, likely the bubonic plague. She died soon thereafter. When undertakers were nailing down the lid of her wooden coffin, it's said that Luther cried out in faith-filled agony, "Hammer away! On doomsday she'll rise again."

People, understandably, respond differently to death: After the death of their brother Lazarus, Martha rushed to Jesus; Mary did not. While Mary grieved, Martha was encouraged by Christ's personal presence. Jesus assured her that not only would her believing brother be resurrected at last, but despite the condition of his body, he remained alive in spirit. Moments later, they both witnessed the miracle of the resurrection of Lazarus.

Faith in Jesus grants confidence in eternal life, even when threatened by the apparent finality of death.

John 11:32–44
Jesus Wept

When Mary came to where Jesus was and saw Him, she fell at His feet and told Him, "Lord, if You had been here, my brother would not have died!"

When Jesus saw her crying, and the Jews who had come with her crying, He was angry in His spirit and deeply moved. "Where have you put him?" He asked.

"Lord," they told Him, "come and see."

Jesus wept.

So the Jews said, "See how He loved him!" But some of them said, "Couldn't He who opened the blind man's eyes also have kept this man from dying?"

Then Jesus, angry in Himself again, came to the tomb. It was a cave, and a stone was lying against it. "Remove the stone," Jesus said.

Martha, the dead man's sister, told Him, "Lord, he's already decaying. It's been four days."

Jesus said to her, "Didn't I tell you that if you believed you would see the glory of God?"

So they removed the stone. Then Jesus raised His eyes and said, "Father, I thank You that You heard Me. I know that You always hear Me, but because of the crowd standing here I said this, so they may believe You sent Me." After He said this, He shouted with a loud voice, "Lazarus, come out!"

The dead man came out bound hand and foot with linen strips and with his face wrapped in a cloth. Jesus said to them, "Loose him and let him go."

It has long been a staple in Bible quizzes: "What's the shortest verse in the Bible?" Hands shoot up, and at least one kid shouts it out before being called on: "Jesus wept!"

This miniscule verse comes right in the middle of the story of Lazarus being raised from the dead. At this point, he's still dead. Jesus had just spoken to Lazarus' sister Martha. Lazarus' other sister Mary is weeping at Jesus' feet, and she's telling Jesus that if He had been there, Lazarus wouldn't be dead. She was heartbroken.

So why did Jesus weep? Scripture doesn't tell us, exactly, but we can take a few guesses. His friends were suffering, and He would have had compassion for them. Even though He knew what was about to happen, they didn't, and they were hurting. He also may have been angry over the reality of death in this world, as a result of our sin. And He knew that He was about to have to die Himself in order to rectify that situation.

Jesus wept with His friends, and He had compassion on them, and He did what only He could have done—He raised Lazarus from the dead. Jesus also weeps with us when we weep, He has compassion on us, and He died and rose from the grave Himself so that we can also be raised from spiritual death. Take a moment to praise Him for that today!

John 14:1–11

The Son Reflects the Father

"Your heart must not be troubled. Believe in God; believe also in Me. In My Father's house are many dwelling places; if not, I would have told you. I am going away to prepare a place for you. If I go away and prepare a place for you, I will come back and receive you to Myself, so that where I am you may be also. You know the way to where I am going."

"Lord," Thomas said, "we don't know where You're going. How can we know the way?"

Jesus told him, "I am the way, the truth, and the life. No one comes to the Father except through Me.

"If you know Me, you will also know My Father. From now on you do know Him and have seen Him."

"Lord," said Philip, "show us the Father, and that's enough for us."

Jesus said to him, "Have I been among you all this time without your knowing Me, Philip? The one who has seen Me has seen the Father. How can you say, 'Show us the Father'? Don't you believe that I am in the Father and the Father is in Me? The words I speak to you I do not speak on My own. The Father who lives in Me does His works. Believe Me that I am in the Father and the Father is in Me. Otherwise, believe because of the works themselves.

Most people have an opinion as to who God is and how He acts in this world. Historically, many people have distorted who He is and have used His name as license for doing some awful things that have tarnished the image of God as well as the reputation of His followers. Because of this and a lack of knowledge of God's Word, many people do not have a clear understanding of who God really is.

In John 14 Jesus made it very clear how we should discern the true image of God. We should look at Jesus. Throughout John's Gospel Jesus identified Himself with the Father. He is the Word of God. He is one with the Father. He does nothing except what the Father does.

Jesus is the perfect reflection of God because He was fully God in human form. Jesus' words and actions are perfectly unified. Together, they define the very nature of God.

Jesus is our true, exclusive window into God's heart. As you seek to know God, look at the heart of His Son. Jesus' life and actions show us who God is, as well as how much the Father loves each and every one of us!

Luke 12:1–3
The Revelation of Light

In these circumstances, a crowd of many thousands came together, so that they were trampling on one another. He began to say to His disciples first: "Be on your guard against the yeast of the Pharisees, which is hypocrisy. There is nothing covered that won't be uncovered, nothing hidden that won't be made known. Therefore, whatever you have said in the dark will be heard in the light, and what you have whispered in an ear in private rooms will be proclaimed on the housetops.

Jesus had just clearly delineated a spiritual principle. More accurate than the law of gravity and more infallible than the law of relativity, here Jesus presents His law of revelation.

Because Christ is Light, His purpose has always been to reveal and uncover by piercing the darkness. He desires to manifest to us the splendid excellence of His glory. His method? To bathe everything in Light.

A room may look elegant and romantic by the flicker of candlelight, but expose it to the brightness of day and all inconsistencies become evident—the cracking paint, the peeling wallpaper, the dingy carpet. What low light masks, the sun's rays accentuate.

Likewise in our lives, fear of exposure may be our greatest dread. Hiding from light is a well-known coping method for concealment of guilt. But we can't stay in the darkness forever. There is "nothing hidden that won't be made known."

It's amazing that people don't understand this principle, especially leaders, both religious and political. But on a regular basis, secrets come to light, and that which was hidden is exposed. Contemporary examples abound; they surface almost weekly. In the digital age, it is difficult to cover up what happens in the dark. Anyone with hacking skills—or sometimes even basic search engine skills—can dig through someone's past and current life to uncover unsavory details that can ruin those people's careers, marriages, and lives.

The people in the Bible were no less apt to cover up their deeds than we are. King David had an affair with Bathsheba and murdered Uriah to cover up the adultery. Judas betrayed Jesus. Peter denied knowing Jesus. Jacob stole Esau's blessing. Moses murdered an Egyptian, and so forth. They were all found out.

We are all prone to be enticed into the trap of secrecy. We say to ourselves, "No one will know." "I can hide this." "It's my secret." "He will never know I bought this." "She will never know I watched this on the Internet." But the truth of this passage is a cautionary tale that proves to be true over and over again. Nothing is secret. Nothing is hidden. The light will shine and reveal it.

But to children of Light, this law of revelation uncovers our weaknesses for what they truly are: the best avenue for His perfect strength. His children come willingly into Light because they realize the spotlight is always upon Him.

Luke 14:25–35
The Cost of Discipleship

Now great crowds were traveling with Him. So He turned and said to them: "If anyone comes to Me and does not hate his own father and mother, wife and children, brothers and sisters—yes, and even his own life—he cannot be My disciple. Whoever does not bear his own cross and come after Me cannot be My disciple.

"For which of you, wanting to build a tower, doesn't first sit down and calculate the cost to see if he has enough to complete it? Otherwise, after he has laid the foundation and cannot finish it, all the onlookers will begin to make fun of him, saying, 'This man started to build and wasn't able to finish.'

"Or what king, going to war against another king, will not first sit down and decide if he is able with 10,000 to oppose the one who comes against him with 20,000? If not, while the other is still far off, he sends a delegation and asks for terms of peace. In the same way, therefore, every one of you who does not say good-bye to all his possessions cannot be My disciple.

"Now, salt is good, but if salt should lose its taste, how will it be made salty? It isn't fit for the soil or for the manure pile; they throw it out. Anyone who has ears to hear should listen!"

Hate your parents? Your spouse? Your children? Was Jesus really teaching that you should neglect your family? No. First, we must understand that the word "hate" does not mean what we think it means. It could be more easily understood in our culture as "love less." So we should love everyone less than God. Our top loyalty should be to Him. Second, Jesus often encountered people who used their family responsibilities as an excuse not to follow Him. He was making a point that this was not acceptable.

But here's where it gets a little bit hairy. It could be possible that God would ask us to leave some of those relationships behind in order to follow Him. It might not be a permanent situation, but then again, it might. In our culture, family is often the end-all, be-all of our existence. We can't imagine ever leaving the ones we love. But contrary to popular belief, family is not "what life's all about." God is. He should be our end-all, be-all. His desires should come first.

Jesus' two short questions illustrate the need for us to "count the cost" and know what we need to do in order to win the battle. We must know the cost and be willing to give it all up in order to follow Christ. Anything less will not do.

Matthew 20:1-16
A Kingdom of Grace

"For the kingdom of heaven is like a landowner who went out early in the morning to hire workers for his vineyard. After agreeing with the workers on one denarius for the day, he sent them into his vineyard. When he went out about nine in the morning, he saw others standing in the marketplace doing nothing. To those men he said, 'You also go to my vineyard, and I'll give you whatever is right.' So off they went. About noon and at three, he went out again and did the same thing. Then about five he went and found others standing around, and said to them, 'Why have you been standing here all day doing nothing?'

"'Because no one hired us,' they said to him.

"'You also go to my vineyard,' he told them. When evening came, the owner of the vineyard told his foreman, 'Call the workers and give them their pay, starting with the last and ending with the first.'

"When those who were hired about five came, they each received one denarius. So when the first ones came, they assumed they would get more, but they also received a denarius each. When they received it, they began to complain to the landowner: 'These last men put in one hour, and you made them equal to us who bore the burden of the day and the burning heat!'

"He replied to one of them, 'Friend, I'm doing you no wrong. Didn't you agree with me on a denarius? Take what's yours and go. I want to give this last man the same as I gave you. Don't I have the right to do what I want with my business? Are you jealous because I'm generous?'

"So the last will be first, and the first last."

Only through a basic understanding of grace (God's unmerited favor) can we begin to grasp the good news of Jesus Christ. Yet grace is so unfamiliar to our daily lives that an act of grace can disturb us, especially when it is granted to someone else.

According to Jesus' parable above, some workers in the vineyard worked all day. Others worked most of the day. Still others worked only the last portion of the day. But the uneven workload wasn't taken into account when wages were paid at the end of the day. Everyone received the same amount. It is not surprising that those who worked the longest complained about it. It wasn't fair!

The master, however, wasn't concerned with what his workers thought was fair. He paid wages based upon his generosity, which was entirely his prerogative, and not upon the production of individual workers. Jesus made it clear that no hierarchy of merit exists in His kingdom, for His is a kingdom of grace.

Only in a kingdom of grace can the last worker of the shift receive the same reward as the first in line. Only in a kingdom of grace can the least be equal to the greatest, the anonymous as important as the popular.

In fact, in Christ's kingdom the "last" and the "first" who sincerely trust in Jesus as Savior and Lord will be equally satisfied, because of their generous Master who doesn't play favorites.

Matthew 22:1–14
Keep Inviting

*Once more Jesus spoke to them in parables: "The
kingdom of heaven may be compared to a king
who gave a wedding banquet for his son. He
sent out his slaves to summon those invited to the
banquet, but they didn't want to come. Again, he
sent out other slaves, and said, 'Tell those who are
invited: Look, I've prepared my dinner; my oxen and
fattened cattle have been slaughtered, and everything is ready. Come to the wedding banquet.'*

*"But they paid no attention and went away,
one to his own farm, another to his business. And
the others seized his slaves, treated them outrageously and killed them. The king was enraged, so
he sent out his troops, destroyed those murderers,
and burned down their city.*

*"Then he told his slaves, 'The banquet is ready,
but those who were invited were not worthy.
Therefore go to where the roads exit the city and
invite everyone you find to the banquet.' So those
slaves went out on the roads and gathered everyone they found, both evil and good. The wedding
banquet was filled with guests. But when the king
came in to view the guests, he saw a man there
who was not dressed for a wedding. So he said to
him, 'Friend, how did you get in here without wedding clothes?' The man was speechless.*

"Then the king told the attendants, 'Tie him up hand and foot, and throw him into the outer darkness, where there will be weeping and gnashing of teeth.'

"For many are invited, but few are chosen."

The baptismal service was over and the pastor, standing in the baptistery, looked heavenward and said, "Lord, it is done as you commanded; yet there is room."

The Lord's grace is so great that His table is never full. There's always room for more. Each Sunday thousands of the Lord's servants stand at the front of His churches and call out to the lost to come forward and take Jesus as their Savior. Missionaries, some of whom are seized and treated outrageously, share this same message around the world.

As the king continued to invite people to his table, so are we to keep inviting the lost to meet our Lord. Those invited to Jesus' table who fail to come will be replaced with others who choose to say yes to His invitation.

The parable is a story, but the invitation is real. If you have not yet done so, you have the opportunity to accept Jesus now and be a guest at His banquet table. If you have accepted this invitation, it is your turn to invite others. Some will refuse to accept, but keep inviting, because others will see the bountiful feast they can enjoy at Jesus' table and accept Him.

Luke 15:11–24
The Father's Love

He also said: "A man had two sons. The younger of them said to his father, 'Father, give me the share of the estate I have coming to me.' So he distributed the assets to them. Not many days later, the younger son gathered together all he had and traveled to a distant country, where he squandered his estate in foolish living. After he had spent everything, a severe famine struck that country, and he had nothing. Then he went to work for one of the citizens of that country, who sent him into his fields to feed pigs. He longed to eat his fill from the carob pods the pigs were eating, but no one would give him any. When he came to his senses, he said, 'How many of my father's hired hands have more than enough food, and here I am dying of hunger! I'll get up, go to my father, and say to him, Father, I have sinned against heaven and in your sight. I'm no longer worthy to be called your son. Make me like one of your hired hands.' So he got up and went to his father. But while the son was still a long way off, his father saw him and was filled with compassion. He ran, threw his arms around his neck, and kissed him. The son said to him, 'Father, I have sinned against heaven and in your sight. I'm no longer worthy to be called your son.'"

"But the father told his slaves, 'Quick! Bring out the best robe and put it on him; put a ring on his finger and sandals on his feet. Then bring the fattened calf and slaughter it, and let's celebrate with a feast, because this son of mine was dead and is alive again; he was lost and is found!' So they began to celebrate."

In television and the movies, fathers often are pictured as aloof, emotionless, poor communicators, judgmental, and sometimes ridiculous. They are constantly getting into situations where they look like idiots. They can't take care of the children without complaining about it and without some sort of mishap. The women don't even trust them to take care of the kids. You watch these men and wonder just how incompetent they can possibly be. And it perpetuates the stereotype of the present-but-mostly-uncaring dad.

Those media stereotypes don't apply to the father Jesus described in this story. The father Jesus described seemed to be on a constant lookout for his lost son. When he saw him still a long way off, he rushed to meet him. He had compassion on him. He threw his arms around him and kissed him. He ordered a feast to be prepared for him. He had no reluctance or reticence. Who could resist such exuberant, unconditional love?

That is the kind of welcome our Heavenly Father has for us when we return to Him. He is looking for us and anxiously waiting. The instant we make a turn in His direction, He is there to receive us. No earthly welcome can compare to the compassionate embrace of our heavenly Father!

Luke 17:1–4

Rebuke and Forgive

He said to His disciples, "Offenses will certainly come, but woe to the one they come through! It would be better for him if a millstone were hung around his neck and he were thrown into the sea than for him to cause one of these little ones to stumble. Be on your guard. If your brother sins, rebuke him, and if he repents, forgive him. And if he sins against you seven times in a day, and comes back to you seven times, saying, 'I repent,' you must forgive him."

Can we be honest with each other? If this verse would stop after "rebuke him," we would all be a lot happier. Your brother-in-law has an affair. Rebuke him. A friend stabs you in the back. Rebuke her. A drunk driver sends your child to the emergency room. Rebuke him. Your pastor is addicted to porn. Rebuke him.

Isn't it easier to rebuke someone than to forgive? Rebuking people allows us to tell them how wrong they are and how much they hurt us, whereas forgiveness requires us to cancel their debt and pardon their action.

Within this command, Jesus tells His disciples to forgive, not in their own time, but when repentance occurs. Taking this command to heart means we must be prepared to rebuke and to restore. Those two things don't seem to go hand-in-hand, but according to Jesus, they do.

What might be even harder is that if the person commits the same sins against us over and over again and repents each time, we must continue to forgive him. And we know from Matthew's gospel that seven times isn't the limit. "Then Peter came to Him and said, 'Lord, how many times could my brother sin against me and I forgive him? As many as seven times?' 'I tell you, not as many as seven,' Jesus said to him, 'but 70 times seven'" (Matt. 18:21–22). Jesus' point here wasn't to put a limit on it but to say that we should forgive indefinitely. There is no limit on the times we should forgive a person.

That is no easy task. Therefore, we need to spend daily time with the Lord, preparing our hearts and walking with Him. When it's time to rebuke, we need to rebuke. When it's time to forgive, we need to forgive. And forgive. And forgive again.

Jesus gave a command, not a suggestion. This may be one of the most difficult commands in all of Scripture, yet it's there and is to be followed. Is there someone you need to forgive? Has someone sinned against you and repented of it, but you have refused to forgive him or her? Search your heart right now, and ask God to give you the strength and ability to forgive that person.

Matthew 22:34-46
Love God and Love Others

When the Pharisees heard that He had silenced the Sadducees, they came together. And one of them, an expert in the law, asked a question to test Him: "Teacher, which command in the law is the greatest?"

He said to him, "Love the Lord your God with all your heart, with all your soul, and with all your mind. This is the greatest and most important command. The second is like it: Love your neighbor as yourself. All the Law and the Prophets depend on these two commands."

While the Pharisees were together, Jesus questioned them, "What do you think about the Messiah? Whose Son is He?"

"David's," they told Him.

He asked them, "How is it then that David, inspired by the Spirit, calls Him 'Lord':

The Lord declared to my Lord, 'Sit at My right hand until I put Your enemies under Your feet'?

"If David calls Him 'Lord,' how then can the Messiah be his Son?" No one was able to answer Him at all, and from that day no one dared to question Him anymore.

Rules are all around us. Most of us grew up with a list of rules in the classroom. We got our driver's licenses and had to follow rules of the road. As adults, we have workplace rules and just common-sense unwritten rules that we must follow. And, of course, there are all the laws of our land that we have to follow. We cannot escape them.

The Old Testament lays out more than 600 laws/rules, and the Pharisees added many more. In Jesus' day, there was a major focus on rules in Jewish life.

Jesus was confronted by a Pharisee, who would have been considered to be a very religious man. In an attempt to discredit Jesus, the Pharisee asked which commandment was the greatest. Jesus boiled them all down to two—to love God and to love people. He said that all other laws and prophetic teachings hinged upon this. The Pharisees had to be shocked and angered by this answer. This man had taken all of the rules and laws that they had so carefully crafted and followed and thrown them out the window. In their place, He said we just needed to do two things.

He then followed up with a question of His own about who they thought the Messiah was and, to put it bluntly, His answer shut them down. Scripture tells us they stopped questioning Him after that. They must have known they couldn't win.

The thing is, we can't win either. Jesus' answer to the question about the greatest commandment poses a problem for all of us, because we don't have it in us to obey it perfectly. But that is what makes the gospel the good news. Jesus loved the Father and loved people so much that He perfectly kept all of the laws, thus making Him a perfect sacrifice. Believers can now stand before God based on Christ's perfect righteousness. We, too, should strive to love God and people like Jesus.

John 14:15–26
The Presence of the Holy Spirit

If you love Me, you will keep My commands. And I will ask the Father, and He will give you another Counselor to be with you forever. He is the Spirit of truth. The world is unable to receive Him because it doesn't see Him or know Him. But you do know Him, because He remains with you and will be in you. I will not leave you as orphans; I am coming to you.

"In a little while the world will see Me no longer, but you will see Me. Because I live, you will live too. In that day you will know that I am in My Father, you are in Me, and I am in you. The one who has My commands and keeps them is the one who loves Me. And the one who loves Me will be loved by My Father. I also will love him and will reveal Myself to him."

Judas (not Iscariot) said to Him, "Lord, how is it You're going to reveal Yourself to us and not to the world?"

Jesus answered, "If anyone loves Me, he will keep My word. My Father will love him, and We will come to him and make Our home with him. The one who doesn't love Me will not keep My words. The word that you hear is not Mine but is from the Father who sent Me.

*"I have spoken these things to you while I
remain with you. But the Counselor, the Holy Spirit—
the Father will send Him in My name—will teach
you all things and remind you of everything I have
told you."*

One of the greatest gifts God has given believers is the presence
of His Holy Spirit. While we see evidence of the Holy Spirit
coming upon Old Testament saints in times of particular need or
calling, Jesus promised His disciples that the Holy Spirit would abide
with them forever. What does this mean for us? Perhaps most important, it means that we are secured by the Holy Spirit until the Day of
Redemption. His presence is a constant reminder that we are God's
children and we need not fear losing our relationship with Him.

But it also has many practical applications for our everyday lives.
Jesus had just said that if we loved Him we would keep His commandments. How can we do that but by the power of the Holy Spirit? Jesus
knew that He was not setting us up for failure, that He was empower-
ing us by His own presence instead. One of the key names given to the
Holy Spirit is that of Counselor. As our Counselor, He will teach us
the truths of God and reminds of what we have read and learned from
His Word.

John 15:1–8
He Is the Vine

I am the true vine, and My Father is the vineyard keeper. Every branch in Me that does not produce fruit He removes, and He prunes every branch that produces fruit so that it will produce more fruit. You are already clean because of the word I have spoken to you. Remain in Me, and I in you. Just as a branch is unable to produce fruit by itself unless it remains on the vine, so neither can you unless you remain in Me.

I am the vine; you are the branches. The one who remains in Me and I in him produces much fruit, because you can do nothing without Me. If anyone does not remain in Me, he is thrown aside like a branch and he withers. They gather them, throw them into the fire, and they are burned. If you remain in Me and My words remain in you, ask whatever you want and it will be done for you. My Father is glorified by this: that you produce much fruit and prove to be My disciples.

In order to make His disciples clearly understand the necessity of maintaining a close relationship with Him, Jesus used the allegory of the vine. The disciples were aware that the vine had become the symbol for the nation of Israel. When Jesus said, "I am the vine," He was agreeing with Isaiah and Jeremiah, who portrayed Israel as a wild and degenerate vine. But Jesus was the true Vine of God.

The disciples would also have been more aware of how grapes are grown than most of us are today. It is a little-known fact that for the first two years after planting a grapevine, most farmers do not allow the vine to produce fruit. The reason for this practice is to allow the plant to develop a strong root system and be sturdy enough to hold the fruit as it grows.

Once the roots are strong, the goal for the vine is to have branches that bear fruit—not just a few little grapes, but large clusters of luscious, mouth-watering fruit that make the taste buds tingle. For this to happen, much pruning needs to be done. Any branch that does not bear fruit is pruned because it is taking nourishment from those that do bear fruit.

Remaining in Christ means we must be diligent in pursuing those things that help us grow. And, just as the farmers prune the grapevines, we must take things out of our lives that divert our focus from Christ. What will you do today to develop deep roots and remain in Christ?

Mark 12:1–12
Our Cornerstone

Then He began to speak to them in parables: "A man planted a vineyard, put a fence around it, dug out a pit for a winepress, and built a watchtower. Then he leased it to tenant farmers and went away. At harvest time he sent a slave to the farmers to collect some of the fruit of the vineyard from the farmers. But they took him, beat him, and sent him away empty-handed. Again he sent another slave to them, and they hit him on the head and treated him shamefully. Then he sent another, and they killed that one. He also sent many others; they beat some and they killed some.

"He still had one to send, a beloved son. Finally he sent him to them, saying, 'They will respect my son.'

"But those tenant farmers said among themselves, 'This is the heir. Come, let's kill him, and the inheritance will be ours!' So they seized him, killed him, and threw him out of the vineyard.

"Therefore, what will the owner of the vineyard do? He will come and destroy the farmers and give the vineyard to others. Haven't you read this Scripture: The stone that the builders rejected has become the cornerstone. This came from the Lord and is wonderful in our eyes?"

*Because they knew He had said this parable
against them, they were looking for a way to arrest
Him, but they were afraid of the crowd. So they left
Him and went away.*

When the great cathedrals were erected, skilled craftsmen and builders were careful to select only the finest and strongest stones to become the cornerstone. A solid foundation was required for these massive structures; anything less would cause the buildings to crumble. The cornerstone was the starting point—the stone upon which and around which the entire structure would be based. If it was not strong and straight, the construction of the entire building would not go according to plan.

Jesus Christ—God's own Son—was rejected and killed by the Jews. And when He hung on the cross and died, there were those who believed He was finished. But He was only beginning to change the world! This rejected stone was lifted up by God Himself to be the Cornerstone of the kingdom of God. What was thought to be weak was, in fact, the strongest, highest, and all-sufficient source of strength for our faith. Jesus is the stone upon which the entire structure of the world is based.

What kind of foundation have you built your life on? Is it rock solid, immovable? Or have you built your life on something that will not hold up under the weight and stand the test of time? Build your life on Jesus, the chief Cornerstone, the only Rock that will stand strong forever.

Luke 19:1–10
A Saved Little Man

He entered Jericho and was passing through. There was a man named Zacchaeus who was a chief tax collector, and he was rich. He was trying to see who Jesus was, but he was not able because of the crowd, since he was a short man. So running ahead, he climbed up a sycamore tree to see Jesus, since He was about to pass that way. When Jesus came to the place, He looked up and said to him, "Zacchaeus, hurry and come down because today I must stay at your house."

So he quickly came down and welcomed Him joyfully. All who saw it began to complain, "He's gone to lodge with a sinful man!"

But Zacchaeus stood there and said to the Lord, "Look, I'll give half of my possessions to the poor, Lord! And if I have extorted anything from anyone, I'll pay back four times as much!"

"Today salvation has come to this house," Jesus told him, "because he too is a son of Abraham. For the Son of Man has come to seek and to save the lost."

Zacchaeus was a wee little man, and a wee little man was he. He climbed up in a sycamore tree for the Lord he wanted to see. And as the Savior passed that way He looked up in the tree. And He said,

'Zacchaeus, you come down! For I'm going to your house today, going to your house today." Chances are, you didn't have to read that whole thing. You saw the beginning, and you started singing it in your head. For those who might not know, it's a very popular children's song. It's a favorite because of the actions that kids can do along with it.

The problem with this song is it doesn't tell the real story about what happened with Zacchaeus. Yes, he was short. But he was also rich. And a cheat. And most people probably didn't like him. Zacchaeus was a tax collector, and in those days, the tax man basically took whatever he wanted, which was typically more than what the government dictated.

It's a shame that the song doesn't go a little further into Zacchaeus's story, because the ending is the best part. Zacchaeus recognized that he was a sinner, and he promised to give back four times more money than he had stolen.

Jesus didn't go to Zacchaeus's house because the man was righteous. He went because Zacchaeus was a sinner in need of grace and salvation. We, too, are sinners in need of grace and salvation. Jesus wants to come to our houses too. Will you let Him in? Will you see your need for Him and repent of your sins?

Luke 20:19–26
Give to Caesar

Then the scribes and the chief priests looked for a way to get their hands on Him that very hour, because they knew He had told this parable against them, but they feared the people.

They watched closely and sent spies who pretended to be righteous, so they could catch Him in what He said, to hand Him over to the governor's rule and authority. They questioned Him, "Teacher, we know that You speak and teach correctly, and You don't show partiality, but teach truthfully the way of God. Is it lawful for us to pay taxes to Caesar or not?"

But detecting their craftiness, He said to them, "Show Me a denarius. Whose image and inscription does it have?"

"Caesar's," they said.

"Well then," He told them, "give back to Caesar the things that are Caesar's and to God the things that are God's."

They were not able to catch Him in what He said in public, and being amazed at His answer, they became silent.

The religious leaders took every chance they could to try to trap Jesus into saying or doing something that would break their laws.

Jesus was often very clever in answering their questions. In this passage, the religious leaders sent a group to try to trip Jesus up by asking if they should pay taxes to Caesar. But this time was a little different than usual. Before asking their question, they actually tried to butter Jesus up with flattery.

Then the leaders asked whether or not they should pay tribute to Caesar by recognizing as lawful the personal (head count) tax with a coin bearing Caesar's inscription. This was an additional tax above the other taxes each Roman citizen was required to pay. If Jesus approved payment of the tax, it would contradict the Law of Moses, which said allegiance was to be given only to God. If He said the tax should not be paid, Jesus could be found guilty of treason.

The answer Jesus gave began with a concrete object. He had them pull out a Roman coin and He asked them whose picture and title are stamped on it. Of course, everyone knew that Caesar's image was on the coin. Then Jesus replied, "Give to Caesar what is Caesar's and to God what is God's." It was more than a thoughtful response. Our willingness to submit to authority magnifies God's greatness because we obey for God's sake, not the government's. When paying taxes, we fulfill what the government requires of us, which honors God.

We read about taxes again in Romans 13: "For government is God's servant. . . . And for this reason you pay taxes, since the authorities are God's public servants, continually attending to these tasks. Pay your obligations to everyone: taxes to those you owe taxes, tolls to those you owe tolls, respect to those you owe respect, and honor to those you owe honor" (vv. 4, 6–7). We honor God when we honor those He puts in authority over us, including our government officials.

Mark 13:9–20
Endure to the End

"But you, be on your guard! They will hand you over to sanhedrins, and you will be flogged in the synagogues. You will stand before governors and kings because of Me, as a witness to them. And the good news must first be proclaimed to all nations. So when they arrest you and hand you over, don't worry beforehand what you will say. On the contrary, whatever is given to you in that hour— say it. For it isn't you speaking, but the Holy Spirit. Then brother will betray brother to death, and a father his child. Children will rise up against parents and put them to death. And you will be hated by everyone because of My name. But the one who endures to the end will be delivered.

"When you see the abomination that causes desolation standing where it should not" (let the reader understand), "then those in Judea must flee to the mountains! A man on the housetop must not come down or go in to get anything out of his house. And a man in the field must not go back to get his clothes. Woe to pregnant women and nursing mothers in those days! Pray it won't happen in winter. For those will be days of tribulation, the kind that hasn't been from the beginning of the world, which God created, until now and never will be again! Unless the Lord limited those days, no one

would survive. But He limited those days because of the elect, whom He chose."

We like to be liked. Being appreciated by others validates our sense of worth and increases our self-confidence. Applause is a potent vitamin. We want people to agree with us and be on our side.

The opposite is also true. Harsh criticism and rejection are like acids thrown on our tender souls. Just a touch of these caustic liquids cause us to feel like nobodies and shrink from bold living.

Following Jesus requires us to draw our worth and confidence from His unfailing love. Therefore, we have the strength to endure onslaughts of disapproval and even rejection.

Jesus warned the disciples that the hostilities coming against Him would come against them. It didn't take long for Jesus' words to be fulfilled. Only a few weeks after Jesus' ascension, the same leaders who crucified Jesus threatened, jailed, and beat His followers.

As we draw our life from Jesus, and not the approval of the world, we will be able to live as devoted followers of Jesus even when others mock, hate, and reject us. We will be able to stand strong during times of trial and tribulation that are to come. Since we are sure of the end, we can find motivation to press on in the midst of the difficult circumstances in which we may find ourselves.

Mark 13:24–31
The Things That Will Last

But in those days, after that tribulation: The sun will be darkened, and the moon will not shed its light; the stars will be falling from the sky, and the celestial powers will be shaken.

Then they will see the Son of Man coming in clouds with great power and glory. He will send out the angels and gather His elect from the four winds, from the end of the earth to the end of the sky.

Learn this parable from the fig tree: As soon as its branch becomes tender and sprouts leaves, you know that summer is near. In the same way, when you see these things happening, know that He is near—at the door! I assure you: This generation will certainly not pass away until all these things take place. Heaven and earth will pass away, but My words will never pass away.

Logic says that when the leaves on the trees begin fading from green into yellow, red, or orange, the days are getting shorter and winter is coming. The world is ordered so that we have constant signs of things to come.

We also know everything is moving toward decay. We try to prevent it. We spend money trying to impede physical decay. We repair things when they wear down or break. If time has taught us anything, it's that nothing lasts forever. The very earth we are standing on is winding down.

Scientists even say that half of the earth's heat is caused by radioactive decay. The fact that our world will someday fade away is actually proof that Jesus' statement about His words is true. What He says will come to pass, and what He says is reliable. Our hearts can turn to doubt easily, but no matter how long we think it is taking for Jesus to keep His Word, He always does.

Today's devotional passage contains powerful statements about Christ's return. Jesus said these reassuring words in response to His disciple's inquiry about the end of the age. He spoke about some of the signs of the times. However, He cautioned them against trying to predict when the end would come, reminding them that no one knew the time—not the angels or even the Son—except the Father.

Sometimes we are so engrossed in the daily grind of life that we fail to give appropriate attention to the things that really matter, to things with kingdom value, to the things of Christ. Our belief that this world is not our home and will pass away should encourage us to look for that which is truly eternal. Only that which is of Christ will last.

We can be certain that the words of the Lord are true and enduring; they will not pass away. Therefore, we should live in anticipation of their being fulfilled. Rather than trying to figure out a time line for Christ's return, we are to live each day as if He were coming at any moment. That is what really matters.

John 15:9–17
Love One Another

"As the Father has loved Me, I have also loved you. Remain in My love. If you keep My commands you will remain in My love, just as I have kept My Father's commands and remain in His love.

"I have spoken these things to you so that My joy may be in you and your joy may be complete. This is My command: Love one another as I have loved you. No one has greater love than this, that someone would lay down his life for his friends. You are My friends if you do what I command you. I do not call you slaves anymore, because a slave doesn't know what his master is doing. I have called you friends, because I have made known to you everything I have heard from My Father. You did not choose Me, but I chose you. I appointed you that you should go out and produce fruit and that your fruit should remain, so that whatever you ask the Father in My name, He will give you. This is what I command you: Love one another.

For Jesus, love wasn't primarily a feeling; it wasn't always best conveyed through words; it was an action. He led His disciples by example. As His life was nearing its end, He gave them this command: "Love one another."

They had seen Jesus play with children. They had watched Him heal countless diseases and infirmities. They had marveled as more than five thousand people ate from a boy's lunch of bread and fish. They had felt His anguish and watched Him weep at Lazarus's grave. They had seen Him raise that same man from the dead. They had seen His tender forgiveness of the woman caught in adultery. They had witnessed His courage as He took on the religious leaders.

Now He gave them a command. He told them to love one another. He had provided the example in His three short years of ministry and He was now telling them exactly what to do. Love with actions, not just words.

Even in His death, which came just a short while after Jesus spoke these words, He chose to die for the benefit of others. No one has ever shown any greater love than this: Jesus laid down His life for sinners. We cannot die for the sins of the world, but we can be willing to love others so much that we would be willing to die for them or give up things that are dear to us for their benefit.

Do you love others? Does that love come through in what you do? Ask God to help you to continue to show more and more love for others through your actions.

John 16:25-33
The Way of Peace

"I have spoken these things to you in figures of speech. A time is coming when I will no longer speak to you in figures, but I will tell you plainly about the Father. In that day you will ask in My name. I am not telling you that I will make requests to the Father on your behalf. For the Father Himself loves you, because you have loved Me and have believed that I came from God. I came from the Father and have come into the world. Again, I am leaving the world and going to the Father."

"Ah!" His disciples said. "Now You're speaking plainly and not using any figurative language. Now we know that You know everything and don't need anyone to question You. By this we believe that You came from God."

Jesus responded to them, "Do you now believe? Look: An hour is coming, and has come, when each of you will be scattered to his own home, and you will leave Me alone. Yet I am not alone, because the Father is with Me. I have told you these things so that in Me you may have peace. You will have suffering in this world. Be courageous! I have conquered the world."

Setting things up to be smooth and trouble-free is impossible for you and me. It won't happen! Isaiah 9:6 foretold Jesus as the Prince of Peace. But how does that mean anything to us right now in our daily lives? Sure, we know that final victory is the Lord's. However, to reconcile what we see going on around us with our belief that He is sovereign and in control is sometimes difficult.

In the devotional passage, Jesus had yet to face the cross and to face the retreat of these now faithful disciples, but He knew it would happen. He knew the agony He was about to endure. He knew what the disciples would soon face, and He knew it would be difficult for them. But He could hold to the fact that God the Father was with Him and that the victory was already His. His disciples could also hold onto that truth, and so can we.

From where do we expect peace to come? Jesus said there will be suffering in this world, and the only peace worth having—and that will be everlasting—comes from a relationship with Him. A relationship with Jesus brings daily encouragement that can overshadow the troubles of our lives. That is the way of peace.

If you have trusted in Christ for your salvation, His peace is available to you. It is there for the taking. If you have not yet made the decision to follow Jesus, know that true peace can only come when you trust in Him. Now is a great time to make that choice!

John 17:20-26
The Church Is One

I pray not only for these, but also for those who believe in Me through their message. May they all be one, as You, Father, are in Me and I am in You. May they also be one in Us, so the world may believe You sent Me. I have given them the glory You have given Me. May they be one as We are one. I am in them and You are in Me. May they be made completely one, so the world may know You have sent Me and have loved them as You have loved Me. Father, I desire those You have given Me to be with Me where I am. Then they will see My glory, which You have given Me because You loved Me before the world's foundation. Righteous Father! The world has not known You. However, I have known You, and these have known that You sent Me. I made Your name known to them and will make it known, so the love You have loved Me with may be in them and I may be in them.

A church was having internal problems. When the pastor and some members of the congregation repented of their sins and unwise choices and sought the forgiveness of others, they were rebuffed. The second group said, "You needn't think that's going to change things!" The second group's sin caused them to refuse to seek unity with their brothers and sisters. Rather than cause a split, the pastor and the first group left and joined other churches in the community.

Soon, the remaining members called a pastor. The man of God moved in, saw all the empty pews, and said, "We need to reach our neighbors."

They scheduled an evangelistic meeting with the new pastor preaching. No one came and no one was reached. The community wanted nothing of what that group had to share.

The greatest reason for unity within the church is so that people may believe in Jesus. Nothing grabs the attention of the world faster than God's people loving each other. Likewise, nothing shuts down a thriving evangelistic outreach faster than disharmony within the Lord's family. The community notices when we do great things, and they notice when we don't. It's foolish to believe the world isn't watching us.

The unity the Lord desires is oneness of spirit, not necessarily organizational unity. We won't always agree with each other, but we can still live in unity and serve each other in love. We should love one another across our denominations, despite our cultural differences, and even over national borders.

Matthew 25:1–13
Be Prepared

"Then the kingdom of heaven will be like 10 virgins who took their lamps and went out to meet the groom. Five of them were foolish and five were sensible. When the foolish took their lamps, they didn't take olive oil with them. But the sensible ones took oil in their flasks with their lamps. Since the groom was delayed, they all became drowsy and fell asleep.

"In the middle of the night there was a shout: 'Here's the groom! Come out to meet him.'

"Then all those virgins got up and trimmed their lamps. But the foolish ones said to the sensible ones, 'Give us some of your oil, because our lamps are going out.'

"The sensible ones answered, 'No, there won't be enough for us and for you. Go instead to those who sell, and buy oil for yourselves.'

"When they had gone to buy some, the groom arrived. Then those who were ready went in with him to the wedding banquet, and the door was shut.

"Later the rest of the virgins also came and said, 'Master, master, open up for us!'

"But he replied, 'I assure you: I do not know you!'

"Therefore be alert, because you don't know either the day or the hour."

It is possible to understand the main point of the parable of the virgins without understanding wedding rituals in the first century, but let's have a quick lesson anyway. The virgins were what we would call bridesmaids. The wedding would start at the bride's house with the bride and her maids in attendance. The groom would arrive and escort her to his home, where the ceremony would be completed. The bridesmaids would go along, and if the wedding were an evening or nighttime event, they would light the procession with lamps (or torches).

Now that you can picture the scene better, the story might make a little more sense. The bridesmaids were waiting at the bride's house, but the groom was late. Apparently all of the bridesmaids had oil in their lamps, but only half of them were prepared for a delay by bringing along extra oil.

One would think that the bridesmaids with oil would just share theirs with the ones who hadn't brought extra. That would be the charitable and compassionate thing to do, right? But remember, this isn't a true story—it's a parable—and compassion isn't the point. Being prepared for the delayed coming of the Lord is the point.

The bridesmaids couldn't share their oil with their friends any more than we can share our salvation with our friends. Each one must prepare on his or her own. Those who have only a little oil—an interest in or knowledge of the gospel—will not be allowed to go with Jesus when He returns. Only those who are fully prepared and true followers will be ready when the groom comes.

Are you fully prepared? If not, remember we "don't know either the day or the hour" when Christ will return. Make the decision to follow Him today.

Matthew 25:14–23
A Faithful Servant

For it is just like a man going on a journey. He called his own slaves and turned over his possessions to them. To one he gave five talents; to another, two; and to another, one—to each according to his own ability. Then he went on a journey. Immediately the man who had received five talents went, put them to work, and earned five more. In the same way the man with two earned two more. But the man who had received one talent went off, dug a hole in the ground, and hid his master's money.

After a long time the master of those slaves came and settled accounts with them. The man who had received five talents approached, presented five more talents, and said, "Master, you gave me five talents. Look, I've earned five more talents."

His master said to him, "Well done, good and faithful slave! You were faithful over a few things; I will put you in charge of many things. Share your master's joy!"

Then the man with two talents also approached. He said, "Master, you gave me two talents. Look, I've earned two more talents."

His master said to him, "Well done, good and faithful slave! You were faithful over a few things; I

*will put you in charge of many things. Share your
master's joy!"*

What does it mean to be a faithful servant? Jesus complimented the servants who took what had been given to them and used it wisely. In the case of this parable, the servants each received some amounts of money. The servants who used his resources in appropriate ways were given more resources to use.

You probably know some five-talent and two-talent people. They exercise their God-given resources, skills, and abilities effectively and productively in kingdom service. We admire their accomplishments, most often by pointing to some measure of increase. We may conclude the greater the increase, the greater the person must be.

The emphasis in this parable is not on the different amounts given to the servants or the amounts of total increase. Rather, Jesus tells the story to urge those who would follow Him to do well, model goodness in character, and exercise faithfulness in their service. The Lord has entrusted to each of us that which we can use in His service. He gives us opportunities to honor Him.

What resources do you have at your disposal that could be used for God's kingdom? Do you have a talent for working with children? Do you play an instrument or sing, or even compose music? Are you good with your hands and able to make repairs? Do you have good organizational skills? Any of those resources could easily be put to use in a local church.

Maybe you don't feel like you have any special talents. Take time to pray and ask the Lord to show you ways in which He has gifted you, and then become a faithful servant as the Lord leads you.

Mark 11:1–11
Hosanna!

When they approached Jerusalem, at Bethphage and Bethany near the Mount of Olives, He sent two of His disciples and told them, "Go into the village ahead of you. As soon as you enter it, you will find a young donkey tied there, on which no one has ever sat. Untie it and bring it here. If anyone says to you, 'Why are you doing this?' say, 'The Lord needs it and will send it back here right away.'"

So they went and found a young donkey outside in the street, tied by a door. They untied it, and some of those standing there said to them, "What are you doing, untying the donkey?" They answered them just as Jesus had said, so they let them go. Then they brought the donkey to Jesus and threw their robes on it, and He sat on it.

Many people spread their robes on the road, and others spread leafy branches cut from the fields. Then those who went ahead and those who followed kept shouting:

Hosanna! He who comes in the name of the Lord is the blessed One! The coming kingdom of our father David is blessed! Hosanna in the highest heaven!

And He went into Jerusalem and into the temple complex. After looking around at everything, since it was already late, He went out to Bethany with the Twelve.

This passage describes the beginning of what we call the Passion Week—the events leading up to and including the crucifixion, death, and resurrection of Jesus. The first thing we see is Jesus demonstrating that His knowledge exceeds that of mere man. He knew where the young donkey would be. We also know from John's Gospel that Jesus told His disciples that riding into Jerusalem on a donkey was a fulfillment of prophecy: "Rejoice greatly, Daughter Zion! Shout in triumph, Daughter Jerusalem! Look, your King is coming to you; He is righteous and victorious, humble and riding on a donkey, on a colt, the foal of a donkey" (Zech. 9:9).

And indeed the people of Jerusalem did rejoice. As Jesus came into town, they spread their robes on the road, signifying that they knew Jesus was royalty. They declared through their words that they knew who was in their presence. The word "Hosanna" is a Greek transliteration of the Aramaic words "Save us, O Lord." At the time, the term was a common one used for a general shout of praise, but the people were unwittingly declaring that this man was the Savior of the World.

Jesus arrived at the temple, and we read in Mark that He left for the evening, but then we see that His next order of business was to clear the temple of those who were using it for their selfish gain instead of revering it as "a house of prayer for all nations" (Mark 11:17).

Jesus made it clear as He entered Jerusalem that He was the Messiah who had come to save the Lord's people. Is that clear to you? Do you believe He is the one who can save you from sin and death? If not, you can make that decision today.

John 12:44-50
We See God

*Then Jesus cried out, "The one who believes
in Me believes not in Me, but in Him who sent Me.
And the one who sees Me sees Him who sent
Me. I have come as a light into the world, so that
everyone who believes in Me would not remain in
darkness. If anyone hears My words and doesn't
keep them, I do not judge him; for I did not come
to judge the world but to save the world. The one
who rejects Me and doesn't accept My sayings has
this as his judge: The word I have spoken will judge
him on the last day. For I have not spoken on My
own, but the Father Himself who sent Me has given
Me a command as to what I should say and what
I should speak. I know that His command is eternal
life. So the things that I speak, I speak just as the
Father has told Me."*

The teacher asked, "What are you drawing?"

"I am drawing a picture of God," the little girl replied.

The teacher gently reproved, "But no one knows what God looks like."

"That's why I am drawing this picture. They will when I am finished."

Some of us, if we are honest, would really like to see that picture of God. Sometimes it seems it would be so much easier to live out the Christian life if we could just see God.

But we can see God. In the passage above, Jesus was speaking to His disciples just days before He was crucified. As He had done many times, He revealed who He was: the Messiah, the Savior of the World. He was the Son of God. God the Father had sent Him to Earth to say and do His will. When we see Jesus, we see God.

And God gave us a vivid picture of His Son in the Gospels. In Jesus' temptation, we see God's perfect holiness lived out in human life. As He cleansed the temple driving out the money changers, we get a glimpse of God's wrath. When we see Jesus embracing children, we see God's loving arms open to all mankind. When we see Jesus teaching His disciples, we see the fullness of God's truth in living flesh. When we see Christ on the cross, we see the full extent of God's grace poured out for fallen humanity. In the resurrection of Jesus, we see God's promise of eternal life.

Just as John fell on his face before the glorified Christ, we too should tremble at His glory. Jesus is God revealed to us. He is Emmanuel, God with us. When we look at Jesus, we see what God is like.

John 13:1–16
Wash One Another's Feet

Before the Passover Festival, Jesus knew that His hour had come to depart from this world to the Father. Having loved His own who were in the world, He loved them to the end.

Now by the time of supper, the Devil had already put it into the heart of Judas, Simon Iscariot's son, to betray Him. Jesus knew that the Father had given everything into His hands, that He had come from God, and that He was going back to God. So He got up from supper, laid aside His robe, took a towel, and tied it around Himself. Next, He poured water into a basin and began to wash His disciples' feet and to dry them with the towel tied around Him.

He came to Simon Peter, who asked Him, "Lord, are You going to wash my feet?"

Jesus answered him, "What I'm doing you don't understand now, but afterward you will know."

"You will never wash my feet—ever!" Peter said.

Jesus replied, "If I don't wash you, you have no part with Me."

Simon Peter said to Him, "Lord, not only my feet, but also my hands and my head."

"One who has bathed," Jesus told him, "doesn't need to wash anything except his feet, but he is completely clean. You are clean, but not all of you."

181

For He knew who would betray Him. This is why He said, "You are not all clean."

When Jesus had washed their feet and put on His robe, He reclined again and said to them, "Do you know what I have done for you? You call Me Teacher and Lord. This is well said, for I am. So if I, your Lord and Teacher, have washed your feet, you also ought to wash one another's feet. For I have given you an example that you also should do just as I have done for you.

"I assure you: A slave is not greater than his master, and a messenger is not greater than the one who sent him."

In ancient times, foot washing was something that was done by a slave for his master, or by a child for his parent, or even a disciple for his teacher. It was not something that a master ever did for anyone else. This is why Peter was so adamant that Jesus would not wash his feet. It was well beneath his standing. But Jesus insisted.

The situation was odd enough that when Jesus had finished, He had to explain what He had done. He leveled the playing field. In His kingdom, masters are no more important than slaves. Disciples are no less important than their teachers. All ought to serve each other in humility.

Are you willing to "wash others' feet," or do you feel that is beneath you? According to Jesus, serving others—no matter who they are—should be beneath no one. If the Son of God could clean the smelly, dirty feet of His disciples, surely we can serve anyone!

Matthew 26:14–25
The Betrayer

Then one of the Twelve—the man called Judas Iscariot—went to the chief priests and said, "What are you willing to give me if I hand Him over to you?" So they weighed out 30 pieces of silver for him. And from that time he started looking for a good opportunity to betray Him.

On the first day of Unleavened Bread the disciples came to Jesus and asked, "Where do You want us to prepare the Passover so You may eat it?"

"Go into the city to a certain man," He said, "and tell him, 'The Teacher says: My time is near; I am celebrating the Passover at your place with My disciples.'" So the disciples did as Jesus had directed them and prepared the Passover. When evening came, He was reclining at the table with the Twelve. While they were eating, He said, "I assure you: One of you will betray Me."

Deeply distressed, each one began to say to Him, "Surely not I, Lord?"

He replied, "The one who dipped his hand with Me in the bowl—he will betray Me. The Son of Man will go just as it is written about Him, but woe to that man by whom the Son of Man is betrayed! It would have been better for that man if he had not been born."

*Then Judas, His betrayer, replied, "Surely not I,
Rabbi?"*
"You have said it," He told him.

I t's hard to imagine that someone who spent three years with Jesus—
watching Him teaching, healing, casting out demons, multiplying
food, turning water into wine, and in many other ways revealing that
He was the Messiah—would betray Him in the end. We know from
Matthew's account that Judas was offered thirty pieces of silver for
this betrayal. There is some debate over exactly how much money
this equated to at the time, or how much it would be worth in today's
money. But we do know that in the Old Testament, thirty pieces of
silver was the payment due to a slave owner when his slave was killed by
another person's livestock. So Jesus was betrayed for the price of a slave.

However, we do know that Judas had a change of mind, though it
was much too late. "Then Judas, His betrayer, seeing that He had been
condemned, was full of remorse and returned the 30 pieces of silver
to the chief priests and elders. 'I have sinned by betraying innocent
blood'" (Matt. 27:3–4). He then went out and hanged himself.

What a tragedy. We have to wonder how things would have turned
out differently if Judas had repented of his act instead of simply feeling
remorseful for what he had done and then taking his own life.

But there's no use wasting time on the "what ifs" in Judas' life, just
like there's no use in pondering the "what ifs" in our own. Instead, let's
make wise, godly decisions in the first place so we won't be tempted to
wonder how things might have been different if we'd only been loyal
to our Lord.

Matthew 26:36-46
As He Wills

Then Jesus came with them to a place called Gethsemane, and He told the disciples, "Sit here while I go over there and pray." Taking along Peter and the two sons of Zebedee, He began to be sorrowful and deeply distressed. Then He said to them, "My soul is swallowed up in sorrow —to the point of death. Remain here and stay awake with Me." Going a little farther, He fell facedown and prayed, "My Father! If it is possible, let this cup pass from Me. Yet not as I will, but as You will."

Then He came to the disciples and found them sleeping. He asked Peter, "So, couldn't you stay awake with Me one hour? Stay awake and pray, so that you won't enter into temptation. The spirit is willing, but the flesh is weak."

Again, a second time, He went away and prayed, "My Father, if this cannot pass unless I drink it, Your will be done." And He came again and found them sleeping, because they could not keep their eyes open.

After leaving them, He went away again and prayed a third time, saying the same thing once more. Then He came to the disciples and said to them, "Are you still sleeping and resting? Look, the time is near. The Son of Man is being betrayed

*into the hands of sinners. Get up; let's go! See, My
betrayer is near."*

No one can read of our Lord's agony in the garden and come away thinking He was play-acting, role-playing, or merely setting an example. This was real life. As He contemplated what lay ahead, His pain was genuine, His agony profound. Luke tells us that an angel came and visited Him to strengthen Him because He was in anguish and "His sweat became like drops of blood falling to the ground" (Luke 22:44).

Had there been any other way to carve out salvation for mankind, surely the Father would have granted it and Jesus would have taken it. Clearly, there was no other way.

The next time you hear someone saying that we get to heaven by our good works outnumbering the bad, remember our Lord in Gethsemane. Had the way to salvation been simply by doing good works, God would have spared Jesus this agony. He might have sent Earth a message saying, "You children be good now!"

The Father's will was for Jesus to go to Calvary and pay the ultimate price for our salvation. His will today is that you and I come to Him through the cross, by the shed blood of the Lord Jesus Christ. Thereafter, His will is that we obey Him, that "His will" be the driving force in our lives.

Matthew 26:47–56
The Power of Jesus

While He was still speaking, Judas, one of the Twelve, suddenly arrived. A large mob, with swords and clubs, was with him from the chief priests and elders of the people. His betrayer had given them a sign: "The One I kiss, He's the One; arrest Him!" So he went right up to Jesus and said, "Greetings, Rabbi!" and kissed Him.

"Friend," Jesus asked him, "why have you come?"

Then they came up, took hold of Jesus, and arrested Him. At that moment one of those with Jesus reached out his hand and drew his sword. He struck the high priest's slave and cut off his ear.

Then Jesus told him, "Put your sword back in its place because all who take up a sword will perish by a sword. Or do you think that I cannot call on My Father, and He will provide Me at once with more than 12 legions of angels? How, then, would the Scriptures be fulfilled that say it must happen this way?"

At that time Jesus said to the crowds, "Have you come out with swords and clubs, as if I were a criminal, to capture Me? Every day I used to sit, teaching in the temple complex, and you didn't arrest Me. But all this has happened so that the prophetic Scriptures would be fulfilled." Then all the disciples deserted Him and ran away.

I t's a spectacularly dramatic scene. There's betrayal, bloody confrontation, and imminent death. There's a kiss, a sword, and a human ear on the ground. It could have come straight out of the latest blockbuster movie—or an episode of a popular reality show.

The crucifixion story had begun. Disciples Peter, James, and John were there when a crowd of armed men—along with one of their former comrades—arrived to arrest Jesus. Peter impulsively grabbed a sword and sliced off a soldier's ear!

Jesus' response was classic: He reminded Peter that His power is limitless. He could have easily asked God for legions of angels for protection. He didn't need Peter's brave ear slicing for defense.

When your life gets dramatic, do you start wielding your own defense weapons like Peter, wildly trying to take things into your own hands? Peter was often brave in the face of adversity, we'll give him that, but he also often didn't understand that he could wholly trust in the power of the One he followed. Jesus had tried to explain to the disciples who He was and what He was there to accomplish, but until they had experienced Jesus' death, burial, and resurrection, they didn't begin to understand what He was all about.

But we know. We've read God's Word. So why do we sometimes forget the extent of Jesus' power? We've read the stories, and we've experienced His power in our own lives, yet somehow we still think we can do something to help Him out.

Let's stop underestimating God's power and remember what He did for us on the cross—and after the cross. That's power we cannot deny.

Luke 22:31–34, 54–62
The Benefit of a Look

"Simon, Simon, look out! Satan has asked to sift you like wheat. But I have prayed for you that your faith may not fail. And you, when you have turned back, strengthen your brothers."

"Lord," he told Him, "I'm ready to go with You both to prison and to death!"

"I tell you, Peter," He said, "the rooster will not crow today until you deny three times that you know Me!" . . .

They seized Him, led Him away, and brought Him into the high priest's house. Meanwhile Peter was following at a distance. They lit a fire in the middle of the courtyard and sat down together, and Peter sat among them. When a servant saw him sitting in the firelight, and looked closely at him, she said, "This man was with Him too."

But he denied it: "Woman, I don't know Him!"

After a little while, someone else saw him and said, "You're one of them too!"

"Man, I am not!" Peter said.

About an hour later, another kept insisting, "This man was certainly with Him, since he's also a Galilean."

But Peter said, "Man, I don't know what you're talking about!" Immediately, while he was still speaking, a rooster crowed. Then the Lord turned

and looked at Peter. So Peter remembered the
word of the Lord, how He had said to him, "Before
the rooster crows today, you will deny Me three
times." And he went outside and wept bitterly.

Peter had such good intentions. He was ready to go to prison or even to die alongside Jesus. He was so confident that it makes his denial all the more heartbreaking. After seeing what was happening to Jesus, he apparently had a change of heart about his declaration.

Nope. He hadn't been with Jesus. He wasn't one of Jesus' followers. He didn't even know what the man was talking about. If this were a movie, at this point we'd expect a grim "dun dun dun" sound effect.

But the actual sound effect was the crow of a live rooster. And it was followed by a look from the man Peter had just denied. Did Jesus give Peter an angry look? Was it full of pity? Or did Jesus give His friend a look of compassion? We don't know. But we do know it cut Peter to his core.

When we deny Jesus, we don't get the benefit of actually having to see His face afterward. You read that right. It would truly be a benefit if we had to look Jesus in the eye after we did something to hurt or betray Him. It would definitely make us think twice before doing anything like it again.

But here's what we know. Even if we deny Him, if we come to Him in repentance, He will restore us, just as He restored Peter (see John 21:15–19). Our sin will not disqualify us from future service or blessings. Just read about Peter's exploits in the book of Acts if you have any doubts about that.

Right now would be a great time to thank the Lord for His grace, mercy, and redemption.

Matthew 27:19-26
The Pressure's On

While he was sitting on the judge's bench, his wife sent word to him, "Have nothing to do with that righteous man, for today I've suffered terribly in a dream because of Him!"

The chief priests and the elders, however, persuaded the crowds to ask for Barabbas and to execute Jesus. The governor asked them, "Which of the two do you want me to release for you?"

"Barabbas!" they answered.

Pilate asked them, "What should I do then with Jesus, who is called Messiah?"

They all answered, "Crucify Him!"

Then he said, "Why? What has He done wrong?"

But they kept shouting, "Crucify Him!" all the more.

When Pilate saw that he was getting nowhere, but that a riot was starting instead, he took some water, washed his hands in front of the crowd, and said, "I am innocent of this man's blood. See to it yourselves!"

All the people answered, "His blood be on us and on our children!" Then he released Barabbas to them. But after having Jesus flogged, he handed Him over to be crucified.

The news commentator states, "Statistics show that most people agree." A teen says, "But everybody else is going." Your business associate explains of a shady business practice, "It's just part of doing business." No matter your age, how do you handle peer pressure? Are you brave enough to stand for right?

The hoax trial for sinless Jesus had spun out of control, and a riot was looming. Pilate, the key leader, seemed to have figured out that Jesus was an innocent man. As he heard the priests, elders, and angry crowds crying out for Jesus' death, however, Pilate folded under peer pressure. He literally washed his hands, declaring his innocence in the matter and pretending that he was not at fault for the decision. Pilate had a chance to stand for Jesus, but he gave in to the crowd.

One could argue that Pilate gets a bad rap. After all, somebody had to make the decision to let an innocent man die in order for Jesus to fulfill His destiny, right? Pilate was just playing his part in God's plan (though he had no idea how massive that plan was). Yes, but there were plenty of people who truly wanted Him to die. Pilate was a man who seemingly didn't care if Jesus died or not. He just wanted the people off his back, so he gave in to their pressure.

You have to wonder what Pilate thought after Jesus rose from the dead. When he heard the news, did he go to his window and yell, "I told you so!"? Was he horrified by the part he had played in this story? We don't know. But we do know what it's like when we give in to the pressure to do something we know isn't right.

When crowds around you are making bad choices, will you join them? Will you allow a herd mentality to choose your direction in life? Or will you wisely and boldly seek God's truth?

Matthew 27:45–54
Unfathomable Love

From noon until three in the afternoon darkness came over the whole land. About three in the afternoon Jesus cried out with a loud voice, "Elí, Elí, lemásabachtháni?" that is, "My God, My God, why have You forsaken Me?"

When some of those standing there heard this, they said, "He's calling for Elijah!"

Immediately one of them ran and got a sponge, filled it with sour wine, fixed it on a reed, and offered Him a drink. But the rest said, "Let's see if Elijah comes to save Him!"

Jesus shouted· again with a loud voice and gave up His spirit. Suddenly, the curtain of the sanctuary was split in two from top to bottom; the earth quaked and the rocks were split. The tombs were also opened and many bodies of the saints who had fallen asleep were raised. And they came out of the tombs after His resurrection, entered the holy city, and appeared to many.

When the centurion and those with him, who were guarding Jesus, saw the earthquake and the things that had happened, they were terrified and said, "This man really was God's Son!"

Think about the most unbearable physical or emotional pain you've ever personally experienced. Imagine the most horrific scene you've ever seen on the news or in a movie. Now breathe. Those events don't come close to this one. It's doubtful that even an actual crucifixion scene from a movie about Jesus can come close to depicting the horror of that experience. After all, we just watch it for several minutes. Jesus lived it for hours.

When we get to this passage, the crucifixion had begun six hours before, and the agony worsened each minute. He'd been tortured and beaten almost to death, then nailed to the cross to die a slow, painful death. Strangers gawked at His naked form. People taunted Him and challenged His seeming lack of power to get down off the cross. Soldiers mocked Him relentlessly and gambled for His clothes. Mark tells us, "Even those who were crucified with Him were taunting Him" (Mark 15:32).

Every breath was difficult. Death was imminent. But Jesus was not only dying—He was dying for our sin. As part of God's salvation plan, Jesus was voluntarily substituting His life for our sins. Your sin. My sin.

Imagine the raw pain in Jesus' voice as He loudly cried from the crucifixion cross, "My God, My God, why have You forsaken Me?" Jesus was quoting from Psalm 22. The entire psalm depicts elements of physical suffering, similar to what Jesus experienced. But He was also expressing the enormous weight of desperation and loneliness as He hung dying, carrying the weight of the world's sin.

We can't fathom the depth of Jesus' pain as He cried out those words. But we can get a small glimpse of His love for us. Let's take time to reflect on all the ways He has shown His love to us.

Matthew 27:62–66; 28:1–6
Christ Is Risen from the Dead

The next day, which followed the preparation day, the chief priests and the Pharisees gathered before Pilate and said, "Sir, we remember that while this deceiver was still alive He said, 'After three days I will rise again.' Therefore give orders that the tomb be made secure until the third day. Otherwise, His disciples may come, steal Him, and tell the people, 'He has been raised from the dead.' Then the last deception will be worse than the first."

"You have a guard of soldiers," Pilate told them. "Go and make it as secure as you know how." Then they went and made the tomb secure by sealing the stone and setting the guard.

After the Sabbath, as the first day of the week was dawning, Mary Magdalene and the other Mary went to view the tomb. Suddenly there was a violent earthquake, because an angel of the Lord descended from heaven and approached the tomb. He rolled back the stone and was sitting on it. His appearance was like lightning, and his robe was as white as snow. The guards were so shaken from fear of him that they became like dead men.

But the angel told the women, "Don't be afraid, because I know you are looking for Jesus who was crucified. He is not here! For He has been resurrected, just as He said. Come and see the place where He lay."

S ometimes those intent on stamping out Christianity end up assisting it. As any high school physics student can attest, fire burns brighter under pressure.

Interestingly, the Lord's opponents remembered that He predicted He would rise from the dead, even if His disciples did not remember.

It appears the wrong guys were taking Jesus' words literally! The disciples, forgetting the Lord's promises, were mired down in their sadness and their grief. Matthew records multiple instances in which Jesus said He would rise gain on the third day. But somehow the disciples didn't get it. It doesn't seem to have occurred to them that Jesus actually might defeat death like He said He would.

When the opponents of the Lord went to such lengths to protect the tomb, they inadvertently provided extra evidence for His resurrection by ruling out all other explanations. Many historians assure us that the only explanation that makes sense and satisfies all the evidence is Jesus Christ rose bodily from the grave!

There are silly theories concocted by people who refuse to believe. Some say He wasn't completely dead to begin with. Others say He faked His death. Anticipating this, Scripture goes to lengths to establish His death and burial, too. It even goes so far as to record the elders' and chief priests' plan to cover up the resurrection with a story about the disciples stealing the body. However, the history is solid; our faith is well-grounded.

Christ was dead. He is risen. He is alive and well today, and He is the Savior of the world!

John 20:24–31
He Lives Within My Heart

But one of the Twelve, Thomas (called "Twin"), was not with them when Jesus came. So the other disciples kept telling him, "We have seen the Lord!"

But he said to them, "If I don't see the mark of the nails in His hands, put my finger into the mark of the nails, and put my hand into His side, I will never believe!"

After eight days His disciples were indoors again, and Thomas was with them. Even though the doors were locked, Jesus came and stood among them. He said, "Peace to you!"

Then He said to Thomas, "Put your finger here and observe My hands. Reach out your hand and put it into My side. Don't be an unbeliever, but a believer."

Thomas responded to Him, "My Lord and my God!"

Jesus said, "Because you have seen Me, you have believed. Those who believe without seeing are blessed."

Jesus performed many other signs in the presence of His disciples that are not written in this book. But these are written so that you may believe Jesus is the Messiah, the Son of God, and by believing you may have life in His name.

Missouri is the "Show Me" state, implying that Missourians are skeptical until physically shown that something is true or real. They have to see it to believe it. Many people have the same view. They take what people tell them with a grain of salt and wait to see the evidence. Frankly, this mind-set can be quite understandable. Perhaps those people have been fooled or deceived too many times, and they don't want it to happen again.

Evidently Thomas had some of that same "show me" tendency. Since he had been absent when Jesus first appeared, Thomas would not believe simply based on the word of others. He wanted to physically see for himself that Jesus was alive. When the Lord appeared a second time, and Thomas saw Him, he exclaimed, "My Lord and my God" (v. 28). However, Jesus said it was better to believe without seeing. This message is great news for us, because we don't have the option of seeing the events of Scripture for ourselves.

While we haven't seen the physically resurrected Christ, we have heard the story from multiple eyewitnesses through the pages of the Bible. We have also experienced the truth that dwells in our hearts. Our lives have been radically changed because of the risen Christ, as have the lives of so many others. A physical appearance would not make Jesus any more real than He is right now. The hymn "He Lives" by Alfred H. Ackley says it this way: "You ask me how I know He lives? He lives within my heart!"

John 21:15–19
Follow Me!

When they had eaten breakfast, Jesus asked Simon Peter, "Simon, son of John, do you love Me more than these?"

"Yes, Lord," he said to Him, "You know that I love You."

"Feed My lambs," He told him.

A second time He asked him, "Simon, son of John, do you love Me?"

"Yes, Lord," he said to Him, "You know that I love You."

"Shepherd My sheep," He told him.

He asked him the third time, "Simon, son of John, do you love Me?"

Peter was grieved that He asked him the third time, "Do you love Me?" He said, "Lord, You know everything! You know that I love You."

"Feed My sheep," Jesus said. "I assure you: When you were young, you would tie your belt and walk wherever you wanted. But when you grow old, you will stretch out your hands and someone else will tie you and carry you where you don't want to go." He said this to signify by what kind of death he would glorify God. After saying this, He told him, "Follow Me!"

When you consider the condition of your relationship with Jesus Christ, you have to ask yourself a very simple question: Do I love Jesus Christ more than anything else? That's the simple substance that is foundational to the relationship. That's the question Jesus was asking Peter.

Jesus led Peter through an experience that would remove the cloud of his denial. Peter had denied Jesus three times after Jesus was arrested and subsequently sentenced to die. A short time later, three times Jesus asked Peter if he loved Him. When Peter answered yes, each time Jesus gave him an instruction. Why? It is one thing to say you love Jesus, but the real test is willingness to serve Him.

Love is the kind of affection that has to be demonstrated, and in our relationship with the Lord it will show up in obedience. When we truly love Him, we will want to please Him and do as He asks.

We know that the two greatest commandments are to love God and to love others. Jesus showed in this passage that when we love God, we must serve others, which is one way we demonstrate our love for both them and for Him.

Three times Peter said that he did not even know the Lord, now three times he said he loved the Lord. No matter how great a person is, he may fall. But God's grace and forgiveness will restore the repentant. At the end of this passage, Jesus said, "Follow Me!" Peter had to have been filled with joy that the One he had betrayed still wanted him to not only serve His followers but also follow Him.

He calls us to follow Him as well, even knowing all the ways we have betrayed Him. Let that knowledge fill you with joy today!

Matthew 28:16–20
Go and Make Disciples

The 11 disciples traveled to Galilee, to the mountain where Jesus had directed them. When they saw Him, they worshiped, but some doubted. Then Jesus came near and said to them, "All authority has been given to Me in heaven and on earth. Go, therefore, and make disciples of all nations, baptizing them in the name of the Father and of the Son and of the Holy Spirit, teaching them to observe everything I have commanded you. And remember, I am with you always, to the end of the age."

We often call this passage the Great Commission. And it might be surprising to some that the term is not found in Scripture. In fact, scholars think it was coined by Dutch missionary Justinian von Welz in the 1600s, and it was popularized in the 1800s by Hudson Taylor, British missionary to China. So Christendom existed for more than sixteen hundred years before this term came about.

Traditionally, the focus has been on the word "Go." Basically, the point is that we are to go into all the world and tell others about Jesus. Mission-sending agencies really like this focus.

However, in the last few decades there has been a lot of press about the idea that verse 19 is not so much about going and more about making disciples. The reasoning behind this is based on the verb tenses of the words. Technically, the only imperative verb (command, for those of you who are many years removed from third grade grammar) is the one translated as "make disciples." The Greek word for "Go" is not an imperative, and therefore many have recently translated it as "As you are going." As a result, the application has been something like, "As you are going about your life, be on the lookout for ways you can make disciples." Sounds pretty good, especially if you're not sold on the idea of going to other nations to be a missionary.

So we have two camps on what it's all about. Is it about going, or is it about making disciples? New Testament scholar Dr. Bob Mounce has some input on that. He argues that the "go" verb, while not an imperative, takes on the mood of the main verb, which makes it act as an imperative. (Google it if you want more explanation.) So, he says, "Jesus' instructions are proactive; we are to move out into the world, not simple [sic] make disciples when we happen to be there."

Now that you've gotten your Greek lesson for the day, let's talk about what this means for us. Are we to go? Yes. Are we to make disciples? Yes. Do we have to go to China or Sudan or Peru to do so? No. But we should be willing to do so. And what can give us the strength to do that? We can look at the final sentence—Jesus' often-overlooked promise: "I am with you always, to the end of the age."

Mounce quote: http://zondervanacademic.com/blog/the-participle-as-imperative.